# Vivisection and Dissection in the Classroom:

## *A Guide to Conscientious Objection*

**Gary L. Francione**
*Professor of Law*
*Rutgers University School of Law—Newark*
Director, Rutgers Animal Rights Law Clinic

**Anna E. Charlton**
*Associate Director, Rutgers Animal Rights Law Clinic*

**About the cover:**

The argument for conscientious objection to vivisection and dissection is rooted in the first amendment to the United States Constitution. Highlighted in the illustration is the third article of the original Bill of Rights, which was eventually adopted as the first amendment.

Published by The American Anti-Vivisection Society, 801 Old York Road, #204, Jenkintown, PA 19046-1685 USA

© 1992 Gary L. Francione and Anna E. Charlton.

Typeset in 11/13 Trump Mediaeval by Kingswood Advertising, Inc., Ardmore, PA. Printed on recycled paper by Tursack Printing, Inc. of Pottstown, PA.

Francione, Gary L., Charlton, Anna E.
Vivisection and dissection in the classroom: a guide to conscientious objection

ISBN 1-881699-00-5 (pbk)
Library of Congress Catalogue Card Number: 92-71852

1. vivisection   2. dissection   3. animals   4. laboratory animals   5. animals' rights   6. animal experiments
7. animals and law   8. animals, treatment of
9. Constitution—first amendment   10. conscientious objection   11. civil rights

Throughout this work, generic pronouns and pronominal adjectives are in the feminine except where quotations use the masculine form. This usage reflects the authors' view that language reflects the racism, sexism, and speciesism of our culture, and that a more careful use of language can only help to raise consciousness about the exploitation of all oppressed groups.

The views and opinions expressed in this publication are those of the authors, and are not necessarily those of Rutgers University, Rutgers Law School, The American Anti-Vivisection Society, or any other institution.

Dedicated to José Ferrater-Mora.

# TABLE OF CONTENTS

# Acknowledgments

This monograph came about as the result of working over the years with students who objected to vivisection and dissection in their course curricula, and who had the courage to do something about it.

My first such encounter involved a lawsuit against the University of Pennsylvania School of Veterinary Medicine on behalf of two veterinary students, Gloria Binkowski and Eric Dunayer. At the time, Penn was still reeling from the scandal involving the Head Injury Clinical Research Center of its School of Medicine, and Robert Marshak, then Dean of the Veterinary School, was not going to let any animal rights activists raise a conscientious objection to the sacred activity of student surgery. Dean Marshak and his staff informed the students that they would be expelled from the school if they refused to perform needless surgery on live, healthy dogs, and then kill those dogs. Gloria and Eric refused, and they received a grade of "F" in the course, which meant that they were not able to continue at the school. With the help of The American Anti-Vivisection Society, the New England Anti-Vivisection Society, and People for the Ethical Treatment of Animals, we put together a legal team and brought suit against Penn. The case was eventually settled in favor of Gloria and Eric, and Penn now offers an alternative for students who do not wish to exploit and kill healthy animals.

Gloria and Eric did not have an easy time. They were harassed by their professors, by Dean Marshak, and even by some of the other students. The going got rough at spots, but both Gloria and Eric persevered and did what they knew was morally right. And they prevailed. Today, Gloria is a practicing veterinarian (and an excellent one, I would add!), and Eric, who also earned his degree, works as a consultant to various animal organizations in addition to practicing veterinary medicine. Gloria and Eric were pioneers—they were people willing to risk the goal that they valued most—to be veterinarians—in order to vindicate their belief in the sanctity of *all* life. I am grateful to Gloria and Eric, and I will always consider them close colleagues in the struggle for animal liberation.

After the Penn case, I began to advise students across the country who wished to object conscientiously to vivisection/dissection requirements. In most of these cases, I was able to negotiate an arrangement morally acceptable to the student. In some other cases, litigation was required. To date, none of the students that I have represented has been dismissed from their educational programs. Eventually, the issue will be decided by the United States Supreme Court, and we will, once and for all, have a definitive ruling on this matter that will apply to *all* states.

This is all by way of saying that my thoughts on the matter of students' rights in the classroom have developed as I have been exposed to different situations that called for different responses. This development has occurred over a period of years, during which I have had the good fortune of receiving assistance from an excellent group of people. My closest friend and spouse, Anna Charlton, Esq., Associate Director of the Rutgers Animal Rights Law Clinic, has consulted with me on every case that I have done and has served as co-author of this monograph. In addition, my student assistants, Roberta DiBiase, Angela DiLeo, Kathleen Gardner, James Kozachek, Mary Jean Pizza, and Claudia Wernick, did a splendid job throughout the process. Wendi Zimmerman, Administrative Assistant of the Rutgers Animal Rights Law Clinic, helped with the manuscript.

John Javes and Bill Stoler of Kingswood Advertising, Inc., and Andrew Clark of Tursack Printing, provided excellent service and stewardship during the design and production phase of this work, which is deeply appreciated.

Special thanks for their support of the Rutgers Animal Rights Law Clinic go to: The American Anti-Vivisection Society, and especially the late Messrs. William Cave and Robert Hudson, who had the insight to recognize the need for this publication; Bob Barker, Nancy Burnet, Sue Coe, Dr. Priscilla Cohn, the late Professor José Ferrater-Mora, Professor Tom Regan and Nancy Regan, Patty Shenker, Doug Stoll, and especially little Molly Brown, and to Tom Regan, Bill Kunstler and Arthur Kinoy for their kind endorsements. Many thanks are due to Bernard Unti of The American Anti-Vivisection Society, who has supported this project strongly, and who has been a longtime ally in the struggle for animal rights. Moreover, Mr. Unti's editorial suggestions helped make the essay more intelligible to lay readers.

Finally, I want very much to acknowledge my non-human companions, Chelsea, the Bandit, Stratton and Emma, who remind me why I get up every morning to fight for animal rights.

Gary L. Francione

# Introduction

*The Importance of the Student Rights Issue*

Whether a student has a right to refuse to participate in the use of nonhumans as part of a course requirement is, strictly speaking, a *civil rights* issue and not an *animal rights* issue. As far as our legal system is concerned, the substance of the belief motivating the student's conduct is—and should be—irrelevant. That is, it should not matter whether the student is objecting to a requirement that she exploit nonhumans, or a requirement that she take an exam on a religious holiday. As long as the student's objection can be phrased so that it falls under the first amendment to the Bill of Rights of our federal Constitution, then our legal system should offer protection to the student even if the system does not yet afford rights to animals.

This is certainly not to say that the animal rights movement should ignore the issue of student rights. Two of the goals of the animal rights movement are to get the legal system acclimated to the concept of animal rights and to raise public consciousness. There can be no doubt that in the past five years, students in grammar schools, high schools, universities and colleges, and professional schools have succeeded in furthering these goals by attempting to vindicate their rights as students to refuse to participate in the exploitation of nonhumans in the classroom.

As our legal system does not yet recognize that nonhuman animals can be the holders of rights, it is necessary to use other means to move our courts toward recognition of animal rights. One such means is to use accepted legal doctrines to highlight indirectly an animal concern. When a student challenges the legality of a requirement that she exploit nonhuman animals, she may be vindicating her own right and not that of a nonhuman, but her action serves to get the issue of animal rights before the court in a civil rights context that is thoroughly familiar to the court. Although it is not necessary for the court to accept the student's view that animals have rights in order for the court to protect the civil right of the student to object, the student has succeeded in raising the consciousness of our judicial system about the underlying issue—animal rights.

*Anytime* a student refuses to be forced to engage in exploitation of nonhumans in the classroom—even when the student does not ultimately bring a lawsuit—the student raises public consciousness about the issue of animal rights. A student who objects may be ridiculed by other students and harassed by instructors. It is clear, however, that at least *some* students and faculty begin to think about the issue of animal rights, perhaps for the first time. And to the extent that the student's challenge is publicized, the public is exposed to the animal rights issue in a most favorable light. Most people recognize that it is not necessary to exploit animals in educational contexts, and they are left wondering why an instructor or institution would attempt to coerce a student into such exploitation. The conclusion that most people draw is an important and correct one: those who exploit nonhumans are often not reluctant to violate the civil rights of humans.

The animal rights movement *must* support those students who are courageous enough to refuse to exploit nonhuman animals in educational contexts. The struggle of these students is the struggle of the animal rights movement.


*What This Book Is—And What It Is Not*

This book is intended primarily as a guide for students who do not wish to vivisect or dissect nonhuman animals used in various educational contexts. In order to provide a thorough explanation of the topic, it is necessary to discuss a number of legal concepts. No one should be intimidated by this material. The concepts are fairly simple, and we have made every effort to explain them in a lucid manner.

In addition, it is incumbent upon *every* activist to develop at least passing familiarity with the law as it relates to those areas of animal protection in which she works. Animal exploiters frequently violate even the minimal legal standards that exist, and, all too often, activists do not utilize these violations effectively because they are unaware of the relevant law.

For example, if the primary focus of one's activism is the use of animals in experiments, one should be reasonably familiar with the provisions of the federal Animal Welfare Act and the implementing regulations. Although most knowledgeable people agree that the federal Animal Welfare Act is woefully inadequate, it is useful in a campaign to be able to allege that the targeted vivisector or institution has violated the law in addition to engaging in conduct that most people find reprehensible on a moral level. Unfortunately, many activists never bother to become familiar with the Act, and they are consequently unable to supplement their campaigns with allegations concerning violations of law.

Similarly, an activist interested in stopping the exploitation of animals used in education—on her own behalf or on behalf of other students—should be reasonably familiar with the law regarding the right of a student to object conscientiously. A working knowledge of basic legal principles will enable a student to present solid arguments to instructors and to school administrators, who are less likely to violate rights of which their students are aware. The primary purpose of this book is to provide the background information necessary to equip the activist with a basic knowledge of student rights.

The secondary purpose of this work is to provide information for lawyers who may be assisting students to resist vivisection or dissection requirements. In many instances, students cannot afford legal assistance and must rely on the good will of attorneys who, while sympathetic to the students' concern for animals, may not be knowledgeable about this area of law. This publication will, we hope, provide basic information to assist such an attorney.

This book is *not* intended as a substitute for legal advice from an attorney who is admitted to practice in your state, and who is familiar with all the relevant facts of your particular case. Nor is this book intended as a scholarly or complete survey of legal principles.

In writing a general introduction to the student rights issue, it is impossible to anticipate the myriad facts that an actual case may involve. It is also impossible to discuss certain differences among the laws of the various states that may have an impact on the resolution of a particular case. Finally, the law changes quickly and sometimes dramatically. This book is based on our view of federal law as it exists today. But the United States Supreme Court has never answered the specific question discussed herein, and it is, therefore, very important to keep abreast of any changes.

In the event that you anticipate having to litigate with an institution in order to vindicate the right to refuse to perform vivisection or dissection, you should seek competent legal help. Moreover, you should make sure that your attorney understands *your* particular beliefs. It is not sufficient merely to consult an "animal rights lawyer." Unfortunately, a number of such lawyers urge students to accept alternatives that may not be morally satisfactory to the student. For example, some lawyers advocate that students should accept the alternative of watching a videotape of someone else dissect a cat. In our view, a videotape of dissection is *not* an alternative to animal exploitation—it is merely a different form of animal exploitation. A basic premise of this work is that as long as the student's claim falls within the scope of the first amendment, the student is entitled to a *nonanimal* alternative. Make sure that you consult an attorney who understands your views, and is willing to conduct the case based on those views.

*The Organization of This Book*

In the first chapter, we will discuss the issue of student rights from the perspective of the first amendment to the federal Constitution. The first amendment guarantees the free exercise of religion and freedom of speech. In Chapter 1, we will introduce the free exercise guarantee in general terms and without much detailed explanation. This introduction will then be expanded upon in Chapter 2.

Following this discussion of the religion portion of the first amendment, we will discuss in Chapter 3 how other doctrines of federal law may be used to support a student's objection to vivisection/dissection. As part of Chapter 3, we will discuss the primary statutory vehicle for raising federal claims in a federal court. In Chapter 4, we will briefly discuss doctrines of state law that may be relevant to the student's claim.

The fifth chapter contains a practical discussion of how a student should approach instructors and other institutional representatives. As part of this chapter, we provide several sample letters that a student may use in raising her objection.

In the sixth chapter, we discuss some arguments that are used by defenders of animal exploitation, and we offer responses to those arguments.

In the seventh chapter, we discuss the distinction between *nonanimal* alternatives and alternatives that may offer some advantages over traditional vivisection/dissection requirements, but that still involve animal exploitation. In many instances, schools may agree to provide "alternatives" that the student initially thinks are acceptable. But if the student, after some reflection, concludes that such options are unacceptable because, although they do not require that the student actually vivisect/ dissect, they do require that the student engage in some other *action* that involves animal exploitation, additional conflict may ensue. It is better that a student enter the situation with a clear understanding of her range of options.

In addition to the seven chapters, there are four appendices. In Appendix I, we provide a selection of cases that concern the freedom of religion guaranteed through the free exercise clause of the first amendment of the United States Constitution. In Appendix II, we provide sample legal pleadings as a reference tool. These are not intended for use as actual pleadings; they are intended only to provide guidance.

In Appendix III, we have provided a copy of a resolution adopted by the American Bar Association/Young Lawyers Division concerning student rights. In Appendix IV, we include the California and Florida laws that guarantee the right of certain students to refuse to vivisect or dissect.

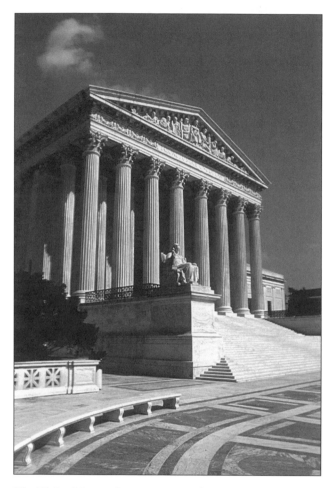

The United States Supreme Court has not yet had to consider a case involving conscientious objection to vivisection or dissection. However, the Court has guaranteed first amendment protection in cases that are relevant to the issue of student rights in the classroom.

# 1

## Student Rights and the First Amendment Guarantee of Freedom of Religion:
### *An Introduction*

### I. The Religion Clauses of the First Amendment

The first amendment to the federal Constitution provides that:

> *"Congress shall make no law respecting the establishment of religion or prohibiting the free exercise thereof . . . "*[1]

There are two prohibitions contained in this clause, and they apply to *both* the federal and state governments. First, the government is prohibited from *establishing* religion. That is, the government may not act in a way so as to show favoritism to any particular religion. For example, the establishment clause would forbid the government from establishing a national religion.

Second, and more relevant for our present purposes, is the *free exercise* clause of the first amendment. The free exercise clause protects our choice to believe in, and to practice, the religion of our choice. As the Supreme Court wrote in 1890: the free exercise clause "was intended to allow everyone under the jurisdiction of the United States to entertain such notions respecting his relations to his Maker and the duties they impose as may be approved by his judgment and conscience, and to exhibit his sentiments in

---

[1] U.S. Const. amend. I.

1

the form of worship as he may think proper, not injurious to the equal rights of others . . . ."[2]

## II. The Distinction Between Belief and Conduct

As the above passage from *Davis v. Beason* indicates, the free exercise clause cannot permit just *any* conduct undertaken in the name of religion. For example, if "one believed that human sacrifices were a necessary part of religious worship, would it be seriously contended that the civil government under which one lived could not interfere to prevent a sacrifice?"[3] Similarly, the courts have held that the sacrifice of animals in religions such as Santeria are not protected by the first amendment.

In interpreting the free exercise clause, the Supreme Court has drawn an important distinction between religious *belief* and religious *conduct*. In *Cantwell v. Connecticut*,[4] the Court wrote that the free exercise clause "embraces two concepts—freedom to believe and freedom to act. The first is absolute but, in the nature of things, the second cannot be. Conduct remains subject to regulation for the protection of society."[5] That is, the government cannot—under *any* circumstances—regulate your religious beliefs or penalize you for your religious beliefs. For example, if the government were to enact a law that made it illegal to believe in the tenets of Hinduism, a state school could not refuse to admit someone on the ground that she believed in those tenets. On the other hand, the government certainly can regulate *conduct*—even if it is characterized as "religious" conduct.

There are two important points to keep in mind concerning the distinction between belief and conduct. First, it is sometimes difficult to distinguish between belief and conduct. For example, when someone refuses to have a blood transfusion on religious

---

[2] Davis v. Beason, 133 U.S. 333, 342 (1890), *overruled*, Thomas v. Review Bd., 450 U.S. 707 (1981).

[3] Reynolds v. United States, 98 U.S. 145, 166 (1879), *overruled*, Thomas v. Review Bd., 450 U.S. 707 (1981).

[4] 310 U.S. 296 (1940).

[5] *Id.* at 303-04.

2

grounds, is that refusal properly characterized as "belief," which cannot be regulated by law, or "conduct," which can be regulated? Is a religious ceremony in itself conduct that can be regulated or merely the collective expression of a commonly held belief? These questions are sometimes very difficult to answer.

Second, and more important, even though the state can regulate religious conduct, there are limits to the state's power. As the Supreme Court has stated: "Where the state conditions the receipt of an important benefit upon conduct proscribed by religious faith, or where it denies such a benefit because of conduct mandated by the religious belief, thereby putting substantial pressure on an adherent to modify his behavior and to violate his beliefs, a burden on religion exists .... [t]he state may justify [such] an inroad on religious liberty by showing that it is the least restrictive means of achieving some compelling state interest."[6]

If we examine the preceding quotation carefully, we can identify the five elements for evaluating the propriety of the regulation of conduct that is claimed to be protected by the first amendment. We will review these elements briefly below, and will then discuss each element in greater detail in Chapter 2.

*There Must Be "State Action"*

It is essential that we have *state action*. That is, there must be some relationship between the government (state, federal, or local) and the challenged activity so that the infringing activity may be treated as that of the state itself. If the entity alleged to infringe upon religious freedom is not a state actor, then the first amendment does not even apply.

For example, if the United States Congress passed a law that prohibited the holding of certain religious beliefs, such action would constitute the action of the state, and those affected could assert their first amendment rights in a court. If, however, your next door neighbor, who is neither an employee nor agent of the state, were to prevent you physically from attending worship ser-

---

[6] Thomas v. Review Board, 450 U.S. 707, 717-18 (1981).

vices, then you would have no lawsuit under the first amendment because your neighbor's activity had nothing to do with the government. You may, of course, be able to sue your neighbor in tort[7] for what is called "false imprisonment," but you could not bring a *first amendment* claim against the neighbor.

### The Belief Must Be "Religious"

It is also essential that the asserted belief be a *religious* belief. That is, the law does not protect bare "ethical" beliefs. On the other hand, the law does not require a belief to be "theistic" or based on faith in a "God" or "Supreme Being." Religions not based on theistic notions are deemed to have equal status under the first amendment. This qualification is particularly important for animal rights activists, many of whom have spiritual beliefs that cannot be regarded as "theistic."

Moreover, it is not necessary that the claimant be a member of a formal religious organization. Again, this qualification is important because many animal rights activists subscribe to a "reverence for life" belief system that does not have a formal institutional existence.

Finally, it is not necessary that the asserted belief be recognized as legitimate by others who may also claim to be adherents to a particular belief system. This qualification is particularly important for those activists who are members of formal religions in which the concept of animal rights is rejected, or, at least, where the acceptance of animal rights values remains controversial. For example, although there is a strong intellectual foundation for asserting that the Judeo-Christian framework can include, and historically has included, respect for animal rights, such respect has been largely suppressed by religious institutions. The fact that your priest, pastor, or rabbi does not share your view that

---

[7] The law of tort concerns non-contractual civil wrongs. For example, if X injures Y as the result of X's negligent conduct, Y would have an action in tort against X because X committed a civil wrong against Y.

your religion encompasses animal rights is, and should be, irrelevant.

## The Belief Must Be "Sincere"

An implied requirement of invoking first amendment protection for religious beliefs is that the claimant be sincere in holding her beliefs. This requirement should not be surprising—it would not make much sense to protect *insincere* beliefs.

## There Must Be a "Burden" on the Free Exercise of Religion

The state must be seeking to impose some sort of *burden* on the exercise of religious freedom. Although there is substantial uncertainty concerning this requirement, it is necessary, at least, to be able to show that the state is trying to condition the receipt of a government benefit on the performance of an act proscribed by the religion.

This is generally not a problem in the present context of student rights. That is, the general scenario is that the state conditions the receipt of a benefit—an education—on the performance of an act—vivisection or dissection—that is proscribed by the student's religious belief system.

## The State Must Have a "Compelling Interest" and Use Narrow Means to Serve that Interest

Once it is determined that the state is burdening the exercise of religious freedom, then the state must prove: (i) that the state's action serves a *compelling* interest, and (ii) that the state is using the least restrictive way of satisfying that compelling interest. That is, not just *any* governmental interest will suffice to justify a burden placed on the free exercise of religion. Rather, the government must have a very important interest that it is seeking to serve, and the government must seek to serve that compelling interest in a consistent way. Consider, for example, a situation in which a school refuses to provide a nonanimal alternative to a student who has a religious objection, but nevertheless allows

5

students who are ill to be exempted from the lab requirement in question. Even if the education of students serves a compelling interest generally, it could hardly be argued that the vivisection/dissection requirement serves a compelling interest in this particular case. After all, if the school does not think that the interest is "compelling" enough to require those who are ill to do the lab on another date, it is unreasonable to argue that the requirement really does serve a "compelling" interest.

Moreover, even if there *is* a compelling state interest at stake, the state must use the least restrictive means possible to satisfy that interest. That is, if there is a way that the state can satisfy an interest *without* infringing upon a student's first amendment rights, then it must do so. For example, if there are nonanimal alternatives to the vivisection/dissection requirement, then the state must use those alternatives rather than requiring the student to do something prohibited by her religious belief.

We will now examine the five elements of a free exercise claim in more detail.

# 2

# Freedom of Religion and Student Rights:
## *A Discussion*

## I. The Five Elements of a Free Exercise Claim

*State Action*

The first element of a free exercise claim is that there be "state action." That is, with the exception of the thirteenth amendment, which forbids slavery and is directed to public *and* private actors, the Constitution protects us only from the action of *government.* This is not to say that there are not other federal or state doctrines that prohibit discrimination on religious grounds by private institutions. As we will discuss later, there are other legal doctrines that may be relevant in a student rights claim. But when we are seeking to assert a *federal constitutional right,* such as the right of free exercise, a court must first decide whether the plaintiff is challenging an action that has been performed by the government.[1]

In most student rights cases, there will be no dispute or issue concerning state action. For example, if a student challenges a federal or state *statute* that requires that all students perform vivisection or dissection as a requirement for graduation, then it is

---

[1] Throughout this chapter, "state action" refers to the action of any level of government—federal, state, or local.

7

clear that the state action element is satisfied. Indeed, when a federal or state legislature, federal or state court, or federal or state executive officer takes some action against a person, that act may generally be challenged under the Constitution. Similarly, when a student sues a *public* grammar or secondary school, or a *public* university or college, on the ground that a vivisection/dissection requirement of a course violates the student's rights, there is generally no problem in holding that state action exists.

The difficult state action issues usually arise when a defendant is ostensibly a *private* actor and it is uncertain whether the defendant can be said to be acting on behalf of the government. In such cases, courts must examine the relationship between the government and the defendant. If the court determines that there is a sufficient connection between the defendant and the government so that the defendant may be said to be acting on behalf of the government, then the court will find that state action does exist, and the defendant's conduct will be subject to scrutiny under constitutional standards. If, however, the court determines that there is insufficient connection, then the plaintiff will be unable to rely on constitutional safeguards.

In the context with which we are presently concerned, *i.e.*, when a student objects to a vivisection/dissection requirement, the state action issue will have two parts. First, as mentioned above, if the educational institution in question is *public*, then the requisite state action is present, and the first element of a free exercise claim is satisfied without further analysis. Second, if the institution is *not* public, then it is necessary to look further to determine whether there is state action even though the potential defendant is ostensibly a private institution. The United States Supreme Court has stated on many occasions that deciding whether state action is present requires "sifting facts and weighing circumstances" on a case-by-case basis.[2] Indeed, the Court has stated that formulating an "infallible test" of state action is

---

[2] *See, e.g.*, Burton v. Wilmington Parking Authority, 365 U.S. 715, 722 (1961).

an "impossible task."[3] Nevertheless, it is possible to isolate two approaches that courts use to determine whether state action is present.

### (a) The Nexus Approach

Most courts recognize that if there is a close connection (or "nexus") between the government's involvement with the defendant and the particular harm being generated, then state action exists. Under the nexus test, courts usually find state action only when the government compelled or encouraged the action that caused the alleged harm. For example, if the state passes a law that *requires* vivisection/dissection as a condition of graduating from any accredited school—public or private, then the state has commanded the very conduct that causes the harm.

Similarly, when state officials or agencies command or encourage the private actor to undertake the harmful conduct, state action exists. For example, assume that a student raises an objection to a vivisection/dissection requirement at a private university, and the dean of that private school calls upon federal education officials for advice as to how to respond. Assume further that these federal officials encourage the dean to refuse the accommodation. In such a case, this encouragement might well serve to satisfy the state action requirement.

In addition, action by a court might well transform an ostensibly private action into state action. In the celebrated case of *Shelley v. Kraemer,*[4] a white person attempted to sell his property to a person of color. The property was subject to a covenant that the owner would not sell the property to minorities, and neighbors sued the white owner to restrain him from violating the covenant and selling to a person of color. The Supreme Court held that if a court were to issue such an order, it would be tantamount to the court ordering the white seller to discriminate against the black

---

[3] Reitman v. Mulkey, 387 U.S. 369, 378 (1967).
[4] 334 U.S. 1 (1948).

buyer.[5] Such a command would violate the Constitution and would certainly constitute state action.

Of these three possible sources of governmental encouragement or requirement, the second (the acts of officials and agencies) holds out the most promise for state action in the vivisection/dissection context. It is well known that federal agencies, such as the National Institutes of Health (NIH) and the Department of Health and Human Services (HHS), endorse vivisection and dissection and respond in a hostile manner toward those who seek to promote animal protection. For example, in May 1984, members of the Animal Liberation Front illegally entered a laboratory at the University of Pennsylvania and removed videotapes, made by Penn experimenters, that depicted horrible cruelty to animals and procedures so sloppy that they virtually guaranteed that any data obtained would be invalid. Instead of condemning the experimenters, or even looking into the matter for purposes of informed comment, Dr. James Wyngaarden, then head of NIH, condemned those who removed the tapes and pronounced that the particular laboratory was "one of the best in the world."

Indeed, it seems as though every time someone criticizes a particular experiment or experimenter, the government immediately launches an attack on the critic. In many cases, the critic may have support from physicians and health care professionals, whose support is simply ignored, or worse still, dismissed without explanation as unsound by government officials and agencies. Further, it is well known that the government has, for years, devoted substantial tax revenues to public relations campaigns designed to encourage a positive image for animal exploitation. Many people, including ourselves, find such government activity outrageous and insulting. However, we also believe that such governmental activity may be transformed into an asset for our movement. The more that the government continues to encourage vivisection and dissection, the easier it will be to trace the seemingly *private* acts of educators and institutions

[5] *Id.* at 20.

10

that require students to exploit animals directly to government encouragement.

Now let us turn to consider some other instances in which the nexus requirement has been discussed in contexts relevant to our inquiry. In *Cohen v. President & Fellows of Harvard College*,[6] a professor claimed that Harvard—a private college—violated his first and fifth amendment rights when the college failed to reappoint him, allegedly in retaliation for his criticism of Harvard's use of federal funds. Cohen argued that his position and research were supported by federal funds and that this created a close nexus between the government and Harvard's failure to renew the contract. The court rejected Cohen's claim, however, holding that the "receipt of government funds does not render the government responsible for a private entity's decisions concerning the use of those funds."[7] The court emphasized that the focus of the nexus test is whether "specific actions of the government . . . in fact motivated the private action"[8] and that Cohen had not proved that the specific actions of the government—the provision of federal funds—motivated Harvard's decision to terminate his employment.

In *Blum v. Yaretsky*,[9] plaintiffs sued a private nursing home on the ground that the transfer of patients to different levels of care without sufficient prior notice constituted a deprivation of due process. The transfers occurred in response to state requirements that physician committees review each patient history, and assign patients to an appropriate level of care. The Supreme Court held, however, that the decisions to transfer the patients were the result of individual medical decisions made by private physicians. The Court reasoned that the state only required that the physi-

---

[6] 568 F. Supp. 658 (D. Mass. 1983), *aff'd*, 729 F.2d 59 (1st Cir.), *cert. denied*, 469 U.S. 874 (1984).

[7] *Id.* at 660 (quoting Genera v. Puerto Rican Legal Services, 697 F.2d 447, 450 (1st Cir. 1983)).

[8] *Id.* at 661.

[9] 457 U.S. 991 (1982).

11

cians make a decision as to care, and could not be held responsible for the actual decision that the physicians made.[10]

The Supreme Court's decision in *Blum* was foreshadowed to a considerable degree by two earlier cases decided by a lower federal court. In *Grafton v. Brooklyn Law School*,[11] two students brought suit claiming that they had been expelled from law school in retaliation for participating in antiwar activities. In trying to establish state action, the students pointed to a number of factors, one of which was that the Commissioner of Education had promulgated certain regulations for law schools. The court rejected this argument, holding that the regulations only required that law schools maintain "a minimum qualitative requirement for graduation."[12] The regulations did not dictate any particular graduation requirement, just as the regulations in *Blum* did not require any particular decision by the physician.

Similarly in *Coleman v. Wagner College*,[13] students brought suit on the ground that they were suspended and expelled for their involvement in a demonstration. The court rejected the argument that a state requirement that all colleges (public and private) promulgate regulations concerning public order on campus gave rise to state action, on the ground that the state requirement did not specify any particular regulations.[14]

Applying these cases to the vivisection/dissection issue, it is clear that if the government prescribes through law or regulation that vivisection or dissection be performed as a prerequisite of graduation, or to satisfy some other requirement, then there is state action. If, however, the state has only a general requirement, *i.e.*, that each student should receive an "adequate" education, then the fact that a private school interpreted this general requirement to mean that students should perform vivisection/dissection in order to get an "adequate" education would not be sufficient to show that the government compelled or encouraged

---

[10] *Id.* at 1004-05.
[11] 478 F.2d 1137 (2d Cir. 1973).
[12] *Id.* at 1141.
[13] 429 F.2d 1120 (2d Cir. 1970).
[14] *Id.* at 1123-24.

the private school to act. If, however, as the result of a legal challenge, a *court* interpreted the general requirement to include vivisection/dissection, then that interpretation would be the same as the state requiring vivisection/dissection explicitly through a law or regulation.

Finally, although it has not yet been tested, an argument may be made that, given the widespread support offered by the government to vivisection/dissection, and the explicit and implicit encouragement of these activities in educational settings, the government *is* encouraging private actors (as well as other public actors) to deny exemptions to students who raise conscientious objections to the exploitation of nonhuman animals.

### (b) The "Interdependence" or "Mutual Contacts" Test

Another approach used by courts to determine whether state action exists focuses not so much on whether the government has compelled or encouraged the private actor to engage in the particular activity, but rather, asks about the extent of contact between the government and the private actor. With this test, we seek to determine whether the government has so "insinuated itself into a position of interdependence with [the entity] that it must be recognized as a joint participant in the challenged activity."[15] This inquiry asks us to judge the extent and nature of the relationship between the government and the private actor. We will now examine certain factors that may inform such a relationship.

*Direct Financial Aid:* The fact that the government has provided financial aid to a private school does not in and of itself mean that the private actor is a state actor.[16] Indeed, small

---

[15] Burton v. Wilmington Parking Authority, 365 U.S. 715, 725 (1961).

[16] In *Grafton v. Brooklyn Law School*, 478 F.2d 1137 (2d Cir. 1973), the plaintiff students also argued that because the state reimbursed the law school $400 for each diploma awarded, the private school was a state actor. The court rejected this argument, but held that if the students claimed racial discrimination (which they did not), then the reimbursement might qualify to trigger state action. *Id.* at 1142-43.

amounts of government subsidy are generally not even a factor militating in favor of state action. Government aid may be relevant to state action *as a factor* when the amount of government aid received is essential to the functioning of the school and the school could not maintain its present level of efficiency or service without it.

For example, in *Rackin v. University of Pennsylvania*,[17] a professor alleged gender discrimination in the tenure process. The court found that extensive subsidy of the *housekeeping* budget of the school, *i.e.*, those funds that may be used for any purpose, can constitute a factor in favor of state action.[18] In *Rackin*, it was demonstrated that the government provided 25% of Penn's operating budget. Similarly, in *Melanson v. Rantoul*,[19] the court held that extensive government subsidy of the *housekeeping* budget is evidence of the required interdependence, but that government subsidies for particular purposes, such as grant money, are not.

Other cases where courts have held that extensive subsidy of *housekeeping* budgets militate in favor of finding of state action include *Braden v. University of Pittsburgh*,[20] and *Isaacs v. Board of Trustees*.[21] In *Braden*, the government provided over 35% of the University of Pittsburgh's budget, and in *Isaacs*, the government provided 54.2% of Temple University's operating income.

Moreover, it is possible to establish financial dependency on the state with evidence other than budget figures. For example, courts often look to the concessions, such as preference in the admissions process for state residents, that state legislatures are able to extract from universities as proof of the interdependent nature of the relationship.

In addition to regarding extensive subsidy of housekeeping expenses as evidence of state action, courts are also willing to support a finding of state action in the case of funds used to subsi-

---

[17] 386 F. Supp. 992 (E.D. Pa. 1974).
[18] *Id.* at 1004-05.
[19] 421 F. Supp. 492 (D. R.I. 1976), *aff'd sub nom. Lamb v. Rantoul*, 561 F.2d 409 (1st Cir. 1977).
[20] 552 F.2d 948 (3d Cir. 1977).
[21] 385 F. Supp. 473 (E.D. Pa. 1974).

dize construction costs. In *Rackin*, for example, the court noted that the Commonwealth of Pennsylvania had provided funds for the construction and financing of various buildings at the University of Pennsylvania and had leased various buildings.[22] In *Braden*, the court noted that between 1966 and 1974, the government had financed the cost of constructing about one third of Temple's buildings.[23]

Having said all this, it is important to be aware that despite past willingness to regard certain forms of direct financial aid as a *factor* in determining the state action question, it is clear that the Supreme Court has become more conservative on the issue. For example, in *Rendell-Baker v. Kohn*,[24] the Supreme Court refused to find state action when a private school for special students, which received virtually all its tuition money from the government, allegedly discriminated against employees. Cases like *Rendell-Baker* seem to indicate that unless the funds are a direct subsidy *to the challenged practice*, the Supreme Court will be reluctant to find state action.

*Indirect Financial Aid:* Generally, courts do not regard indirect aid, such as tax exemption or student loans, as militating in favor of a finding of state action.[25] The reason for ignoring indirect aid is that many libraries, art galleries, and private foundations receive indirect aid (such as tax exemptions), and courts are unwilling to expand that widely the concept of state action.

*Government Regulation:* Many courts have recognized that state regulation of a private school is a factor that may support a finding of state action. However, as the Supreme Court held in *Rendell-Baker v. Kohn*,[26] a government regulatory scheme will generally support a finding of state action only if it is discovered

---

[22] 386 F. Supp. at 998.

[23] 552 F.2d at 961.

[24] 457 U.S. 830 (1982).

[25] Although indirect aid was mentioned as a factor in *Rackin, supra,* the presence of numerous other factors buttressing the finding of state action tends to deflect attention from this factor.

[26] 457 U.S. at 841-42.

that the regulation sanctioned, encouraged, or commanded the challenged practice.[27]

*Receipt of Charter from the Government:* Courts are in general agreement that the fact that a school receives its charter from the government does not signal a metamorphosis of private action into state action. The fact that an entity receives its charter from the government places it on a par with any private corporation, and these corporations surely do not lose their identity as private actors simply because they receive government charters.

*Composition of the Board of Trustees:* The presence of government officials in university positions or on a University's Board of Trustees, or the fact that the government officials are given a role in appointing university officials or trustees, may serve as a criterion of state action. Whether this factor supports a finding of state action is, like other factors of the state action inquiry, a context-sensitive, factually based inquiry. In *Melanson*, the court held that the presence of four state officials on the Board of Trustees of a private college did not suffice to constitute state action.[28] On the other hand, the court in *Rackin* did find state action where 13 members of a 25 member Board of Trustees were public officials.[29]

*Receipt of Benefits of Government's Eminent Domain Powers:* Under the power of eminent domain, a state or local government may take land upon the payment of just compensation. This transaction can occur (and usually does occur) when the state wants land that an owner is unwilling to sell. Courts may be inclined to find state action when the government takes property by eminent domain and then transfers that property to private actors. For example, in *Rackin*, the court acknowledged that a

---

[27] Related cases: Public Utilities Comm'n v. Pollak, 343 U.S. 451 (1952)(government regulation of transit company subjects company to constitutional restraints); Moose Lodge Number 107 v. Irvis, 407 U.S. 163 (1972)(private club not subject to constitutional restraints merely because government granted a liquor license); Jackson v. Metropolitan Edison Co., 419 U.S. 345 (1974)(regulation of monopoly by government does not support finding of state action).

[28] 421 F. Supp. at 497 (D. R.I. 1976).

[29] 386 F. Supp. at 996 (E.D. Pa. 1974).

private university made ample use of lands taken by the Commonwealth through eminent domain and then transferred to the university.[30]

*"Symbiotic" Relationship:* This category is really a "catch-all" that seeks to identify instances where a "totality of circumstances" indicates to a majority of Supreme Court Justices that there is some mutually beneficial relationship between the private actor and the government. For example, in *Burton v. Wilmington Parking Authority,*[31] a privately owned restaurant that rented space in a municipal parking garage discriminated on the basis of race. Although the government did not compel or encourage this discrimination, the Court held that by leasing the parking space, the government gave the impression of approving the discrimination and benefited from the presence of the restaurant. The Court concluded that "the state has so far insinuated itself into a position of interdependence with [the restaurant] that it must be recognized as a joint participant in the challenged activity."[32] Of course, the restaurant was not really a "joint participant" with the government, but the mutual benefits derived from the operation of the restaurant coupled with the public ownership of the building led the Court to treat the private actor and government as though they were actually "joint participants."

*A Note of Caution:* Finally, it should be noted that even if the receipt of state benefits (financial or otherwise) does not subject the private entity to constitutional restraints, the private actor may still be unable to continue receipt of the subsidy. In order to understand this clearly, assume that a private university discriminates against students on the basis of religious beliefs. Assume further that the only connections between the university and the government are: (1) that the state education department has granted accreditation to the university; and (2) that the government provides water, sewage, and other services to the university. In such a case, the university would not, without more, be a state

---

[30] *Id.* at 1001.
[31] 365 U.S. 715 (1961).
[32] *Id.* at 725.

actor. Now assume that the government provides special aid to the university in the form of financing the construction of university buildings, and then leasing space in those buildings in order to help the economic health of the university. Under *Rackin* and other older, lower federal court cases, this additional factor would militate in support of state action. Under *Rendell-Baker* and similar cases, it is not clear how this factor should be weighed. But it is clear, however, that even if the additional *specialized* aid (beyond the provision of *generalized* services such as water, sewage, etc.) is not enough to constitute state action, it may be possible to stop the government from continuing this specialized subsidy to the private offender.

*To Sum Up:* If the institution involved is a public grammar school or high school, or a state college, university, or professional school, then the state action requirement is satisfied, and this portion of the inquiry is at an end. If, however, the institution involved is private, then it is necessary to find state action before constitutional constraints may be imposed on the private actor. The fact that the school receives governmental subsidies or is regulated by the government will probably not suffice.

Under the "nexus" approach, if you can show that the challenged activity—the imposition of the vivisection/dissection requirement over a claim of religious freedom—is compelled or encouraged by the government, then state action may be found.

As we mentioned above, a possible approach to satisfy the nexus requirement would be to argue that the government, through agencies such as the Department of Health and Human Services and the NIH, actively encourages and, in fact, may be said to "require" institutions to respond with hostility to the assertion of claims by animal rights advocates. It was reported some time ago that the NIH was seeking to penalize institutions that "succumb" to pressure from animal rights people. The incident that triggered this NIH response occurred when Cornell Medical School returned a grant for vivisection to the NIH after powerful criticism by animal rights advocates.

Whether the NIH actually does impose penalties of any sort on an institution like Cornell, or on the vivisector involved in the experiment, is not crucial. What *is* very important, however, is

18

that the NIH has already made it crystal clear that it, as a government actor, is outwardly hostile to the animal rights movement and to anyone who responds affirmatively to the ideas of the movement. A biology professor who permitted students who objected to have a nonanimal alternative to a vivisection/dissection requirement could reasonably fear that her accommodation of animal advocates could have a very negative impact on her career as far as government grants are concerned. It is precisely this sort of conduct by the NIH that might prompt a progressive court to find that the government has, in essence, compelled or encouraged the challenged activity, *i.e.*, the refusal to accommodate the student.

Under the "mutual contacts" approach, it is necessary to find interdependence between the government and the private actor. Receipt of any government money by the private actor will generally not be enough. Obviously, the more contacts you can establish, the better. Moreover, it is better if you can show that any government subsidy received by the private actor can be linked to the challenged activity. For example, if the school receives government funds specifically to help finance laboratory facilities, or the lab exercise to which you object, then it is more likely that a court will find the requisite state action.

### "Religious" Belief

As mentioned in Chapter 1, the first amendment does not protect what might be characterized in ordinary language as an "ethical" or "moral" view alone. On the other hand, first amendment protection is not limited to protecting only those who subscribe to belief in traditional religions. Indeed, the scope of protection offered by the first amendment is quite broad, and can easily accommodate the beliefs of most animal rights activists.

Before we discuss the concept of "religious belief" in detail, we offer some preliminary reflections. There are many animal rights activists who label themselves as not religious, or even as anti-religion. A number of animal advocates that we know have rejected traditional religions as involving institutions that are sexist, racist, homophobic, and speciesist and that reflect and serve a selfish and narcissistic society. On the other hand, most of these same animal advocates possess a deeply spiritual commitment to justice for the oppressed and a general revulsion toward violence against sentient beings. Further, these spiritual beliefs have a profound influence over the way that these animal advocates lead their lives. In many respects, their belief in justice for *all* beings has a profound impact on the way that they live their lives day to day—perhaps even more profound than the impact felt by those who go to church once a week and who often pay mere lip service to the ideals preached at their places of worship. In any event, before you regard yourself (or others) as non-religious or even anti-religion, think about the nature of your own beliefs and the impact that they have on your life. As you read what follows, you may be surprised to learn that the first amendment is broad enough to protect a non-traditional, non-theistic philosophy of reverence for life.

In order to simplify the presentation of this material, we want to focus on three situations that are typical of those presented in the student rights context. First, we will consider the case of someone who subscribes to a traditional religion, and whose animal rights views are not accepted by the "mainstream" members of the religion. Second, we will consider those who have theistic beliefs, but who are not members of a particular church or institution or are members of a non-traditional religion. Third, we will consider the case of someone whose animal rights views are not grounded in a theistic doctrine, and whose "religion" may be considered as related to a "reverence for life" philosophy.

## (a) The Non-Traditional Traditionalist

To a greater or lesser extent, a large number of animal rights advocates are practicing members of an organized religion. That is, some activists have "lapsed" somewhat in their formal worship habits, but nevertheless consider themselves to be members of the faith in which they were raised or that they adopted at some point in their lives. Other activists are diligent in their observance of their religion. What is common to both the observant group and, for want of a better expression, the more or less lapsed group, is that both regard their animal rights views as an integral part of their religion.

The problem raised here is what happens when these adherents clash with other members of their religion who do not accept animal rights as part of the religion's doctrine, and who may even be highly offended by the articulation of animal rights views as part of the religion. If no one else in the religion accepts the animal rights view, is the articulation of that view as something that is compelled by the religion still entitled to first amendment protection?

The answer is plainly "yes." The first amendment protects non-traditional beliefs that are expressed as part of traditional religions. That is, if, as Christian, Jew, or Moslem, you regard animal rights as part of your religious tradition, then your animal rights views are generally protected by the first amendment despite the fact that you are the *only* member of your congregation to subscribe to animal rights, and the fact that your co-worshipers regard your animal rights beliefs as ill-founded and perhaps even in contradiction to the fundamental tenets of the religion. Courts dislike—for good reason—deciding whose interpretation of religious doctrine is right and whose is not.

The key case in this area is the Supreme Court's decision in *Thomas v. Review Board*.[33] Thomas was a Jehovah's Witness who quit his job in a machinery company when he was transferred from the roll foundry to a department that produced turrets for military tanks. Thomas claimed that his religious beliefs forbade him to produce war materials. The State of Indiana, where Thomas lived, refused him unemployment benefits and Thomas sued, claiming that the first amendment protected his decision not to work on producing tank turrets.

The U.S. Supreme Court agreed with Thomas. In the opinion, the Court noted that Indiana had refused to accept Thomas' claim, in part, because other Jehovah's Witnesses did agree to work on the tanks, thus making such work "scripturally" acceptable in contradiction to Thomas' position. The Supreme Court

---

[33] 450 U.S. 707 (1981).

rejected that reasoning, holding that "[i]nterfaith differences of that kind are not uncommon among followers of a particular creed, and the judicial process is singularly ill equipped to resolve such differences."[34]

*Thomas* provides very strong support indeed for the proposition that a non-traditional belief expressed by someone in the context of a traditional religion *must* be respected even if other adherents do not subscribe to the same view. This is not to say that a court may not examine a belief in the context of pertinent theological literature and history in order to determine whether it is, indeed, a "religious" belief.[35] In our case, we may simply take note of the growing body of literature by people such as Dr. Michael W. Fox,[36] Rev. Dr. Andrew Linzey,[37] and Dr. Tom Regan[38] that establish clearly that respect for animal life is a tenet of *all* traditional religions. A person may ultimately fail to convince other adherents that animal rights should be a fundamental of the religion as popularly practiced, but that failure has no bearing whatsoever on the constitutional status of animal rights as a protected part of the religious views of someone who subscribes to the animal rights position.

Another very important aspect of *Thomas* involved a claim that Thomas contradicted his expressed views about opposition to the making of war products because he admitted that he would not be opposed to the making of the steel that would ultimately be used for the turrets as long as he was not forced to work on the turrets themselves. In denying Thomas benefits, the Indiana court found that Thomas's views were inconsistent and that Thomas could not really articulate his views with great precision. The Supreme Court rejected this reasoning too, and held that

---

[34] *Id.* at 715.

[35] *See, e.g.,* Quaring v. Peterson, 728 F.2d 1121 (8th Cir. 1984), *aff'd sub nom.* Jensen v. Quaring, 472 U.S. 478 (1985); Stevens v. Burger, 428 F. Supp. 896 (E.D.N.Y. 1977).

[36] M.W. Fox, *High School Dissection of Animals: Ethical and Religious Considerations* (unpublished paper).

[37] A. Linzey, *Christianity and the Rights of Animals* (1987); A. Linzey, *The Status of Animals in the Christian Tradition* (1985).

[38] *Animals and Christianity* (A. Linzey & T. Regan eds. 1988).

"Thomas drew a line [between producing the steel and working on the turrets] and it is not for us to say that the line he drew was an unreasonable one."[39] In addition, the Court added that "[c]ourts should not undertake to dissect religious beliefs because the believer admits that he is 'struggling' with his position or because his beliefs are not articulated with the clarity and precision that a more sophisticated person might employ."[40]

These portions of the *Thomas* decision are particularly important for students who object to vivisection/dissection on first amendment grounds. Frequently, defenders of animal exploitation will reject claims of protected belief by a student, pointing to some other aspect of her behavior as an indication that the student is "inconsistent" in her views. For example, we remember speaking to one vivisector about our student client, who objected to a vivisection requirement. The vivisector claimed that our client's animal rights views about vivisection were not entitled to first amendment protection because she wore leather shoes. *Thomas* precludes precisely this type of argument. That is, *Thomas* allows the believer to draw the line *where she chooses*.

This is not to say that courts cannot inquire into the *sincerity* of a belief, and that inconsistencies might not have a bearing on such an inquiry. For example, if the student operated a private vivisection laboratory to earn tuition for school, and performed numerous animal surgeries on "experimental" animals, it would be difficult for her to draw a line at the very same act (vivisection) occurring in a slightly different place (a veterinary school). But such an inquiry goes directly to the question of sincerity, and that is a separate issue (see below). As long as the student has *sincerely* drawn the line between vivisection and leather shoes, then that is the end of the matter.

In addition, it is important to note that *Thomas* holds explicitly that a person who struggles with her religious beliefs and who may be unable to articulate those views in a completely coherent fashion may still be said to have a sincere claim. This is a very

---

[39] 450 U.S. at 715.
[40] *Id.*

important point for the student who objects to vivisection/dissection. For example, another veterinary student whom we represented had raised an objection to doing a procedure on an "experimental" animal, but stated initially that he would do the procedure as long as the animal was under anesthesia. Later, when the student objected to doing the procedure *at all* because his animal rights thinking had become more progressive, the vivisectors had a field day pointing to the student's allegedly inconsistent behavior. Again, *Thomas* is important. The first amendment does, and must, allow "breathing space" for a person to develop her ideas about her relationship to God (whichever one or ones that might be). The fact that a student changes her position is not determinative of the first amendment question.

This is not to say that shifting positions is a good idea from a strategic point of view; it is not. The more you change your position, the more your antagonists will attempt to argue that your basic belief is insincere. Also, a judge or jury may form a negative impression of you if you are seen as "flighty" and this will very likely have a negative impression on their perception of your cause. The message: changing your view toward a more radical one is acceptable, but it is preferable to be careful and think before you speak in the first instance!

### (b) The Non-Traditional Non-Traditionalist

Some animal rights activists may subscribe to a theistic religion—*i.e.*, one that involves a personal God or supernatural deity—but a religion that is not traditional in the sense of its being a socially recognized religion. The Supreme Court has held that a belief may be "religious" even when it is not part of a recognized religion.[41] If a person has a sincerely held belief in a God or Gods, and believes sincerely that the deity requires non-violence toward animals, then that is the end of the matter.

---

[41] *See, e.g.*, Frazee v. Illinois Department of Employment Security, 489 U.S. 829 (1989).

24

For example, in *Frazee v. Illinois Department of Employment Security*,[42] the plaintiff claimed that although he was not a member of an organized religion, he nevertheless believed that the Bible revealed that work on Sunday was prohibited. The Supreme Court found that the belief merited protection because a belief need not be found in a dogma or tenet of a religious sect in order to obtain first amendment protection.[43]

### (c) The Non-Theist

The third category of persons may, for many animal rights activists, be the most important. Many activists do not belong, or consider that they belong, to any organized or established religion. Moreover, many activists do not believe in a personal God in the way in which Christians, Jews and Muslims do. A number of belief systems that are and must be considered as religions do not have a notion of a personal God or supernatural deity. Rather, some people "think of religion as a way of life envisioning as its ultimate goal the day when all [people] can live in perfect understanding and peace. There are those who think of God as the depth of our being; others, such as the Buddhists, strive for a state of lasting rest through self-denial and inner purification; in Hindu

---

[42] *Id.*

[43] *Id.* at 835. In *Society of Separationists, Inc. v. Herman*, 939 F.2d 1207, 1215 (5th Cir. 1991), the court held that a potential juror had the right to refuse to take an oath or make an affirmation that did not refer to God if such an affirmation was a religious statement for her. The judge's attempt to force the potential juror to take an affirmation violated the free exercise clause. "While the religious connotations of an oath probably seem stronger to most observers, this is not license to dismiss [the potential juror's] view of affirmations as unentitled to Free Exercise protection." *Id.* at 1216. What is a nonreligious act for one person may have profound spiritual dimensions for another. A claim that is not "bizarre [or] clearly non-religious in motivation," *id.* at 1215, is entitled to free exercise protection, even though it may not be "acceptable, logical, consistent or comprehensible to others," *Thomas*, 450 U.S. at 714, as courts may not evaluate religious truth.

philosophy, the Supreme Being is the transcendental reality which is truth, knowledge, and bliss."[44]

A claimant's belief *need not be theistic* in order to receive first amendment protection. That is, the belief does *not* need to be based on God or some other supreme being. This is extremely important to animal rights advocates because many people in the movement do not believe in any notion of a personal God, but nevertheless have a deeply held spiritual belief in the sanctity of life, and reject speciesism on the basis of more than some isolated moral belief.

The Supreme Court has recognized that religions founded on beliefs other than the existence of a personal God have equal status under the first amendment. In doing so, the Court has developed what might be called a "functional" definition of what constitutes a religion. That is, the Court has recognized that in order to determine whether a set of beliefs constitutes a religion, the appropriate focus is not the *substance* of a person's belief system (*i.e.*, whether a person believes in a personal God of the Jewish, Christian or Muslim traditions), but rather, what *function* or *role* the belief system plays in the person's life. It is important that the belief in question be part of a person's "ultimate concern."[45]

The key case in this area is *United States v. Seeger.*[46] In *Seeger*, the Supreme Court faced the issue of whether an individual qualified for conscientious objector status under the draft law by virtue of "religious training and belief"—the statutory grounds for objector qualification—even though he himself explicitly disavowed a belief in God. Seeger stated that his was a "belief in and devotion to goodness and virtue for their own sakes, and a religious faith in a purely ethical creed."[47]

---

[44] United States v. Seeger, 380 U.S. 163, 174-75 (1965), *overruled by* Welsh v. United States, 398 U.S. 333 (1970).

[45] *See, e.g.*, Dettmer v. Landon, 617 F. Supp. 592 (E.D. Va. 1985), *aff'd in part, vacated in part*, 799 F.2d 929 (4th Cir. 1986), *cert. denied*, 483 U.S. 1007 (1987).

[46] 380 U.S. 163 (1965), *overruled by* Welsh v. United States, 398 U.S. 333 (1970).

[47] *Id.* at 166.

The Court held that Seeger's belief did qualify as religious, stating that "[t]he test might be stated in these words: a sincere and meaningful belief, which occupies in the life of its possessor a place parallel to that filled by the God of those admittedly qualifying for the exemption."[48] Although the Court in *Seeger* was construing a federal statute (the Selective Service or draft law), the case is read as "addressing Constitutional limits inherent in the draft statute; the case is, therefore, applicable to First Amendment analysis generally."[49]

Several years later, the Supreme Court relied on *Seeger* in another conscientious objector case under the draft statute, *Welsh v. United States.*[50] In *Welsh*, the Court confirmed that "the central consideration in determining whether . . . beliefs are religious is whether these beliefs play the role of a religion in the [person's] life."[51] The Court went on to describe the role that traditional religions play in the lives of individuals: "Most of the great religions of today and of the past have embodied the idea of a Supreme Being or of a Supreme Reality—a God—who communicates to man in some way a consciousness of what is right and should be done, of what is wrong and therefore should be shunned. If an individual deeply and sincerely holds beliefs that are purely ethical or moral in source and content but that nevertheless impose upon him a duty of conscience . . . those beliefs certainly occupy in the life of that individual 'a place parallel to that filled by . . . God' in traditionally religious persons . . . His beliefs function as a religion in his life."[52]

*Seeger* and *Welsh* not only embrace the psychological function test as a means of discerning the "religious" nature of belief; they also signal and approve the erosion of any "bright line" distinction between "religious" beliefs (as traditionally understood) and ethical or moral beliefs. This is not to say that a "purely secular"

---

[48] *Id.* at 176.
[49] Callahan v. Woods, 658 F.2d 679, 683 n.4 (9th Cir. 1981).
[50] 398 U.S. 333 (1970).
[51] *Id.* at 339.
[52] *Id.* (citing *Seeger*, 380 U.S. at 176).

belief,[53] or "personal codes of conduct that lack spiritual import"[54] would qualify as protected. Rather, if the belief is not rooted in theism of one sort or another, then it will qualify for protection only if it plays the same role in the life of the believer as would a theistic belief or belief system. The belief must go to the person's "ultimate concern" in life. A federal district court in Virginia stated the issue in this way: "Because the concept of a 'religious belief' cannot be defined (and thereby limited) with any real precision, courts must accept a belief as 'religious' so long as it is sincere, it occupies a meaningful position in the individual's life, and it relates to that individual's 'ultimate concern.' An individual's concerns must be described as 'ultimate' when they go beyond purely intellectual matters of self-interest and touch concerns that are in some sense 'spiritual.'"[55]

The evidence to support a claim under this "ultimate concern" analysis would be found in the way in which a claimant leads her life. For example, a belief in the sanctity of all living beings, which manifests itself in the form of a "religious" adherent who is : (1) a vegetarian or vegan; (2) an animal rights activist; and who (3) does not wear leather, fur, or wool, or use personal care products tested on nonhumans, would, in all likelihood, satisfy the "ultimate concern" test. That is, a person whose lifestyle is governed by a strong belief that humans and nonhumans should peacefully coexist without exploitation could show that her belief is the "ultimate concern" of her life.

The above is intended as an example only. There are no doubt many other indicators that a belief or belief system addresses a person's "ultimate concern." These indicators include, but are certainly not limited to, relationships with companion animals, past activities involving animals (i.e., working at a refuge or shelter), academic activities (writing papers concerning animal rights

---

[53] Wisconsin v. Yoder, 406 U.S. 205, 215 (1976).
[54] United States v. Kuch, 288 F. Supp. 439, 443 (D.D.C. 1968).
[55] Dettmer v. Landon, 617 F. Supp. at 595.

28

or environmental ethics), and other evidence that demonstrates the importance of the belief to the claimant.

\* \* \* \* \* \* \* \* \* \*

Two final points to keep in mind: *First,* the "reverence for life" philosophy that many animal rights advocates adhere to is an ideology that may stand alone as a "religion" even though the person does not believe in a God or Gods, and even though the person does not subscribe to any "traditional" religion. Many animal advocates, however, overlook the fact that a "reverence for life" ethic is a basic principle of many traditional religions although those religions may not emphasize the principle. As Dr. Michael W. Fox describes it, "reverence for life and respect for the sanctity of being are beliefs that are shared by many regardless of their affiliation with any formal religion or denomination. *And yet by the same token, reverence for life and respect for the sanctity of being are basic ethical and moral principles of all the world's religions.*"[56] Passages from the Bible (Ecclesiastes and Isaiah) and the Koran, as well as the teachings of Buddha, Gandhi and others, illustrate unequivocally that all the traditional religions have strong strains of reverence for life philosophy, even if the modern practice of these religions fails to reflect this fact.[57]

When you seek to analyze the character of your own beliefs to determine whether they are "religious" in nature, keep in mind that a non-theistic ideology of reverence for life may constitute a "religion" just as a traditional religion that you may practice may contain a reverence for life component of which you were unaware.

*Second,* if you have a valid free exercise claim, then you are entitled to a nonanimal alternative even if other student objectors

---

[56] M.W. Fox, *High School Dissection of Animals: Ethical and Religious Considerations* 3-4 (unpublished paper)(emphasis added).

[57] *See generally id.; see also Animals and Christianity* (A. Linzey & T. Regan eds. 1988).

are willing to settle for less. There are some students who object to vivisection/dissection who may accept "alternatives" that are not *nonanimal* alternatives. For example, a student who objects to dissection on religious grounds may not object to watching someone else do the very same dissection that she refuses to do. We have even seen literature from an animal "rights" group that suggested that students watch videotapes of animals being experimented on as an alternative to doing that type of experiment.

Exploitation is exploitation. Watching someone else do vivisection/dissection is really no different from doing it yourself in an important sense: one of the primary purposes of objection to vivisection/dissection requirements is to affirm the view that the exploitation of nonhumans is *wrong*. Vivisection/dissection is not made any less exploitative because someone else does it. This is not to say that some nonanimal alternatives that still involve some animal use may not offer advantages. For example, if an institution allows a student to watch a videotape of "dog lab" rather than to actually vivisect/dissect the dog, then one more life has been saved. But the alternative is not a nonanimal alternative.

Do not be confused or misled. If other students are willing to accept an alternative with which you are not comfortable, you are entitled to an alternative that fits *your* religious beliefs.

## Sincerity

In order for a student to obtain first amendment protection, it is necessary that her religious beliefs (broadly defined as above) be *sincere*. It should, of course, come as no surprise that the law will not protect a free exercise claim on the part of someone who does not sincerely believe in the claim that she is making.[58] Whether a student's claim is sincere is essentially a question of fact that must be resolved on a case-by-case basis.

For the most part, many of the criteria that suffice to show that a belief is sincerely held will be the very same criteria that a

---

[58] *See* United States v. Seeger, 380 U.S. at 185; United States v. Ballard, 322 U.S. 78 (1944).

TABLE 1

# The Five Elements of a Free Exercise Claim

**1. State Action** (page 7)

There must be *state action*, the revealing of some relationship between the government (federal, state or local) and the challenged activity so that the infringing activity may be treated as something undertaken by the state itself.

---

**2. Religious Belief** (page 19)

The belief in question must be a "religious" belief, i.e., one that is a deeply held belief or part of a comprehensive belief system.

---

**3. Sincerity** (page 30)

The belief that is expressed or asserted by the conscientious objector must be shown to be a *sincere* belief, one that is held genuinely and earnestly.

---

**4. Burden** (page 33)

It must be shown that the state-imposed requirement constitutes a true burden on the conscientious objector, such that it actually infringes on her religious freedom.

---

**5. Compelling State Interest/
Least Restrictive Alternative** (page 34)

There must be a balancing of the conscientious objector's interests against the interests of the government. If the government does burden an admittedly religious belief by requiring the student to engage in an action that is inimical to the student's religious beliefs, the government must be able to point to a *compelling interest* that justifies the burden, and demonstrate that the burden imposed represents the *least restrictive means* of satisfying that compelling interest.

claimant will point to in order to demonstrate that a non-theistic belief constitutes a "religion," *i.e.*, that a non-theistic belief serves essentially as an "ultimate concern" of the claimant's life. For example, the fact that a student is vegetarian, does not wear leather or fur, and the fact that she is willing to risk inevitable retaliation by those hostile to her claim suffice to show *both* that the student's belief encompasses an "ultimate concern" and is sincere as well.

The question of sincerity is arguably a separate inquiry when the claim is made as part of a traditional religion. For example, if a student attributes her opposition to vivisection/dissection to her Christian or Jewish religious beliefs, then, of course, there is no need to determine whether the belief is part of the student's "ultimate concern" because, by definition, the student's adherence to a recognized theistic religion represents an "ultimate concern" of the student. Although there would be no need to ascertain whether the student's belief was "religious" in nature, it would be necessary to ascertain that the student's admittedly religious views were held sincerely. A court would then, as part of a separate inquiry, look to the day-to-day behavior of the student in order to ascertain that the admittedly religious belief was also sincere. For example, the fact that a student was a vegetarian would indicate sincerity.

An important indicator of the sincerity of a belief should be the fact that the student is objecting to the requirement in the first place. Anyone who has ever objected to a vivisection/dissection requirement knows only too well that even if the student succeeds in getting the institution to offer a nonanimal alternative, there will still be "penalties" to pay. That is, the biomedical establishment is extremely hostile to students who are identified with the struggle for animal rights. Accordingly, a student who objects may be "marked" for purposes of future harassment. For example, we once represented a student who succeeded in getting a nonanimal alternative to a dissection requirement, but who then was virtually ignored by many of her former professors for the duration of her stay in the school. Whether courts will accept that the student's sincerity is demonstrated by the very claim that she is making, and by what she is willing to endure to assert and defend that claim,—and that no more indicators of sincerity are necessary—remains to be seen.[59]

## Burden

The next requirement of a free exercise claim is that the state-imposed requirement impose an actual burden on the claimant's religious freedom. The best way to describe this requirement is to discuss a case in which a court found that the state activity argued by the plaintiffs to infringe their free exercise of religion did *not* impose the required burden. In *Mozert v. Hawkins County Board of Education*,[60] schoolchildren and their parents complained that the reading program of the school impermissibly burdened their religious belief. The court held that there was no burden imposed on the children by requiring them to be exposed to ideas to which they may have religious objections. The court stated that "[i]t is clear that governmental compulsion either to do or refrain from doing an act forbidden or required by one's religion, or to affirm or disavow a belief forbidden or required by one's religion, is the evil prohibited by the Free Exercise Clause."[61] That is, if the government requires that a student be exposed to *ideas* that the student may find objectionable on religious grounds, but does not require that the student affirm the truth of those ideas, or *act* in ways inimical to her religious beliefs, then the first amendment free exercise clause is not even triggered.

The U.S. Supreme Court has not yet spoken to the issue raised in *Mozert*, which was decided by a lower federal court. It is unlikely, however, that the presently constituted Supreme Court would find the *Mozert* analysis objectionable. Even if the *Mozert* analysis is ultimately accepted by the Supreme Court, it should

---

[59] A claimant's willingness to accept the consequences of standing by her beliefs, including the inconvenience of litigation, has been recognized by at least one court as some evidence of sincerity. *See* Stevens v. Berger, 428 F. Supp. 896, 901 (E.D.N.Y. 1977).

[60] 827 F.2d 1058 (6th Cir. 1987), *cert. denied*, 484 U.S. 1066 (1988).

[61] *Id.* at 1066.

have no effect on the type of student rights claim being discussed here. When a student is required to vivisect or dissect a nonhuman animal, the student is not merely being exposed to ideas with which she may disagree; rather, she is being asked to engage in an *act* that violates her religious freedom. Unless there is a drastic change in first amendment analysis at the Supreme Court level, there should be no doubt that a vivisection/dissection requirement would constitute the requisite burden needed to trigger first amendment analysis.[62]

## Compelling State Interest/Least Restrictive Alternative

The final requirement that a student must satisfy in order to prevail in this type of case involves a "balancing" of the student's interest against the interests of the government. That is, if the government does burden an admittedly religious belief by requiring the student to engage in an action that is inimical to the student's religious beliefs, the government must be able to point to a *compelling* interest that justifies the burden, and demonstrate that the burden imposed represents the *least restrictive means* of satisfying that compelling interest.[63] If the government cannot demonstrate that there is a compelling interest in the imposition of the burden, or if the government cannot show that the burden represents the least restrictive way of satisfying its compelling interest, then the restriction must fall. Courts are supposed to scrutinize strictly the government's reasons for imposing the burden, and to strike down the government burden if the government cannot meet its obligation to demonstrate the presence

---

[62] For a discussion of the "burden" element in first amendment free exercise claims, see Lupu, *Where Rights Begin: The Problem of Burdens on the Free Exercise of Religion*, 102 Harv. L. Rev. 933 (1989).

[63] There are many Supreme Court cases that discuss the compelling state interest/least restrictive means test. *See, e.g.*, Hernandez v. Commissioner, 490 U.S. 680, 700 (1989); Hobbie v. Unemployment Appeals Comm'n, 480 U.S. 136, 141 (1987); United States v. Lee, 455 U.S. 252, 257-58 (1982); Thomas v. Review Board, 450 U.S. 707, 718 (1981); Wisconsin v. Yoder, 406 U.S. 205, 215 (1972).

of a compelling interest and the absence of a less restrictive alternative.

Although the law is moving in a more conservative direction, it is still safe to offer this guide: if the student succeeds in convincing a court that her objection to vivisection/dissection is based on a sincere religious belief (broadly understood as discussed above) and that the vivisection/dissection requirement does, indeed, burden the exercise of religion, it will be difficult for the government to satisfy the compelling state interest/least restrictive alternative requirement.

We will discuss the compelling state interest/least restrictive alternative test in three specific educational contexts—compulsory education (grade schools and secondary schools), higher education (colleges and universities), and professional school (medical schools, dental schools, and veterinary schools). We will then discuss briefly two points that are important for any inquiry into the state's interest in requiring vivisection/dissection.

(a) Compulsory Education

There is no doubt that the government has a compelling interest in education that it deems *compulsory*. That is, with respect to that level of education that the state requires of all children (*i.e.*, to age 16, through completion of secondary school, etc.) the state clearly does have an interest in inculcating in youth that information which facilitates their participation in a democratic society.[64] In the context of science education, the state has an interest in ensuring that students have the scientific knowledge necessary to function in an increasingly technological society. Although the government clearly has a compelling interest in compulsory education, and although the government may even have a compelling interest in ensuring that students have a basic knowledge of biological science and the functioning of organisms, it is highly doubtful that the state has *any interest whatso-*

---

[64] *See, e.g,* Ambach v. Norwick, 441 U.S. 68 (1979).

*ever* in requiring that students engage in vivisection/dissection in light of the many less restrictive alternatives that exist, such as computer software, realistic models, diagrams, and text book illustrations and explanations. That is, the only conceivable and legitimate pedagogical goal of dissection at the grammar school/high school level is to teach gross anatomy and basic biological functions, and there can simply be no serious argument that these goals must be achieved through the vivisection/dissection of a nonhuman. These goals may be achieved through the use of a nonanimal alternative, and, therefore, the state's interest in biological education, even if compelling, cannot be said to override the student's first amendment rights.

There is a final point to be made here concerning the state's compelling interest in compulsory education. To the extent that the state has such an interest—and it undoubtedly does—parents also have a fundamental right to direct the education of their children, especially where religious doctrines are concerned.[65] This right should not be underestimated. To the extent that a student's parent shares and supports her conscientious objection to vivisection/dissection, the student's case is much, much stronger because her first amendment right, which, in itself, is strong, is combined with yet another very potent fundamental right belonging to the parent. This "combination" right should be invoked in appropriate cases.

### (b) Higher Education: Colleges and Universities

At the college/university level, there is a serious question about whether the state has a compelling interest *at all* in the content of the curriculum. That is, the reason the state has a compelling interest in compulsory education is that compulsory education, which, by definition, is mandatory, is intended to prepare children and adolescents to become productive members of

---

[65] *See, e.g.*, Wisconsin v. Yoder, 406 U.S. 205 (1972)(invalidating compulsory school attendance laws as applied to Amish parents who refused on religious grounds to send their children to school).

36

society. Since no state requires a student to pursue higher education, and since a student who attends a college or university is usually not even required to take biology, it is difficult to argue that the state has *any* compelling interest in a vivisection/dissection requirement at the college/university level.

College/university education is an option that some people choose and others do not; it can hardly be argued that higher education is necessary to fulfill the state's desire to prepare people for citizenship. Indeed, given the diversity of educational institutions and programs, and the principle of academic freedom that protects the right of an instructor to present material in the way that she chooses, the state has virtually no control over the curriculum, as it does in the case of compulsory education.

Even if, contrary to common sense, the state did have a compelling interest in higher education, the broad range of nonanimal alternatives in the case of a vivisection/dissection requirement would prevent any state interest from overriding the student's first amendment rights.

## (c) Higher Education: Professional Schools

Again, it is difficult to argue that the state has any compelling interest in the curriculum of a medical school, dental school or veterinary school. As in the case of colleges/universities, the state exercises little, if any, control over professional school curricula, which are determined by the faculty of the schools.

There is, however, a sense in which the state's interest in professional school education is arguably "more" compelling than the state's interest in college/university education. Specifically, medical, dental and veterinary schools produce health care professionals, and the state is arguably interested to ensure that these professionals are trained in an acceptable way. If doctors, dentists and veterinarians are not trained properly, they will be unable to deliver quality health care, which is undoubtedly important.

Of course, the same may be said of the state's interest in the curricula of beauty schools and trade-training programs. If beauticians and plumbers are not properly trained, people's appearances will be unacceptable and their pipes will leak and cause damage to their homes. But no one (we suspect) would characterize as "compelling" the state's interest in the curricula of its beauty schools and plumbing programs. Similarly, the characterization as "compelling" of the state's interest in the curricula of professional schools is problematic.

Again, even if the state's interest in professional school curricula were considered as "compelling," the presence of nonanimal alternatives renders *any* vivisection/dissection requirement a more restrictive way of achieving the desired goal. A number of medical and veterinary schools in the United States have already eliminated mandatory vivisection/dissection requirements, and such events demonstrate the complete lack of necessity of such requirements.

(d) Two Common Points: Administrative Costs and Motivation

There are two very important points to keep in mind in *any* inquiry into the state's interest in requiring vivisection/ dissection in the classroom. *First*, when a student asks for an alternative, the school almost invariably asserts administrative efficiency as a compelling interest at stake. That is, the school argues that if the alternative is provided, it will create administrative burdens that will threaten the orderly operation of the school.

It is clear—and it is clear beyond doubt—that a state's interest in the avoidance of an administrative burden becomes compelling only when that burden presents administrative problems of such magnitude as to render the operation of the school unworkable.[66] Moreover, the burden is on the state to show that accommodating the student would create unworkable problems.[67] When an

---

[66] *See* Sherbert v. Verner, 374 U.S. 398, 408-09 (1963).

[67] *Id.* at 407; *see also* Quaring v. Peterson, 728 F.2d 1121, 1127 (8th Cir. 1984)(no evidence in record to support state's assertion that exempting a claimant, who objected, on religious grounds, to having her picture taken for a driving license, would lead to exemptions on demand and jeopardize administrative efficiency), *aff'd*, Jensen v. Quaring, 472 U.S. 478 (1985).

administrator tells a student, "we cannot give an exemption because there would be chaos if every student asked for one," or "the cost of the exemption will be too expensive," it is up to the administrator to prove these assertions *and* to show that any burdens will be very, very serious. *It is not up to the student to disprove what the administrator claims.*

*Second*, keep in mind that in virtually every case in which an institution denies an exemption, that denial will be predicated *not* on the sincere belief of the faculty member(s) that there really is no alternative. Rather, the decision is more likely to be predicated upon the fact that the professor/instructor and her colleagues *are opposed to the animal rights beliefs of the students.* That is, if you and your lawyer dig deeply enough, you will find that the school does not really perceive a compelling interest in the vivisection/dissection requirement, but rather, that the school finds compelling its need to maintain the status quo and to fight the animal rights movement at every turn. Once you can identify any such sentiment—and we assure you that it has been there in every case that we have seen to date—then any claim of compelling interest will be discredited to a greater or lesser degree.

## II. A New Twist?

In the preceding section, we explored the five elements of a free exercise claim. It is necessary to point out that this discussion is based on legal precedent—primarily from the United States Supreme Court—that existed before the Court in 1990 decided a case entitled *Employment Division v. Smith.*[68] Although it is too early to tell, *Smith* may change in some ways the framework discussed above. It is important to understand *Smith* and the possible ways in which it may represent an alteration of the Court's framework for analysis of free exercise claims.

Before *Smith*, many courts thought that *every* state-imposed restriction on the free exercise of religion necessitated analysis

---

[68] 494 U.S. 872 (1990).

under the framework discussed above. That is, *anytime* the state was deemed to burden the free exercise of religion, the state had to prove that the burden satisfied a compelling interest and that the state was using the least restrictive means of satisfying that interest. In *Smith*, the Supreme Court held that this approach is not applicable to *all* cases concerning the free exercise of religion.

In *Smith*, two employees, Smith and Black, both of whom were members of the Native American Church, were fired from their jobs at a private drug rehabilitation program because they used the hallucinogenic drug peyote for religious purposes at their church. The first concern that should arise in your mind is that the dismissal, in and of itself, could not trigger the first amendment because the employer was a *private* program, and, therefore, *not a state actor.* (If this thought did not occur to you, go back and read the sections on "state action.")

The state action came into play when Smith and Black sought unemployment benefits from the State of Oregon, and were denied those benefits. The state refused the benefits because Smith and Black, according to the state, were fired for work-related "misconduct," and the state provided employment benefits only for those who lose their jobs through no fault of their own.

Although the Oregon court held that peyote use was illegal in Oregon, and that the criminal law proscribing peyote did not contain an exemption for religious use, it found that the criminal law could not be applied to Smith and Black because the law itself violated their right of free exercise of their religion. That is, the Oregon court held that as long as Smith and Black used peyote only as part of the practice of their religion, the police could not arrest Smith and Black or prosecute them for peyote use. Accordingly, the Oregon court held that the State of Oregon could not deny Smith and Black unemployment benefits because their use of peyote as part of their religion could no longer be considered "misconduct." In reaching these conclusions, the Oregon court relied on the compelling state interest/least restrictive alternative test.

The United States Supreme Court reversed the Oregon court and held that the criminal law prohibiting the use of peyote could be applied to Smith and Black without violating their first amendment rights. According to the Supreme Court, as long as the law in question—in this case, the criminal law prohibiting peyote use—does not have as its goal prohibiting the exercise of religion, then the fact that the *incidental* effect of the criminal law is to prohibit the exercise of religion does not trigger first amendment scrutiny *at all*. It is, therefore, not necessary to apply *any* first amendment analysis.

That is, the Supreme Court explicitly refused to apply the compelling state interest/least restrictive alternative test discussed above. Rather, the Court held that as long as the law in question is a generally applicable criminal prohibition, then the first amendment does not even come into play, and the law will simply be upheld as an exercise of the state's police power.

To use another example, consider the fact that there are many people in this country who practice Santeria and other religions that employ animal sacrifice as part of religious practice. These sacrifices involve the brutal slaughter and torture of nonhumans. Every state has a statute that makes cruelty to an animal a criminal offense, and it is clear that these statutes are not directed in any way against Santeria or other religions, but are simply intended to prevent humans from inflicting cruelty on nonhumans. To the extent that state humane officers enforce anticruelty statutes against practitioners of Santeria, there can be no doubt that such enforcement has an *incidental* effect on the practice of animal sacrifice. But the statutes in question are *neutral* and, the state humane officers are not enforcing the anti-cruelty statutes against the Santeria practitioners *because* they are killing animals in connection with religion, but because they are killing animals. The law is, and should be, indifferent to the *reason* for the killing.

Under *Smith*, the state is not required under such circumstances to demonstrate that it has a compelling interest in animal cruelty and that its prohibition of the practice of animal sacrifice is the least restrictive way of satisfying that compelling interest. Rather, *Smith* holds that the first amendment does not even come into play—no one is entitled to an exemption from the anticruelty laws, even if she claims that exemption in the name of religion.

For our purposes, the most important question raised by *Smith* concerns the scope of the Court's decision. If *Smith* is concerned only with the analysis of a generally applicable criminal prohibition that had only an *incidental* effect on the exercise of religion, then *Smith* will have no effect on the framework discussed above. That is, students who object to vivisection/dissection in the classroom are not, like the Native Americans in *Smith*, requesting an exemption from a generally applicable criminal prohibition that has an incidental effect on religious freedom. There is no law (at least not yet!) that makes it a crime not to vivisect or dissect. Rather, the student who objects to vivisection/dissection is making a different statement: she is saying that the state cannot condition a benefit (an education in biology, for example) on the student's performing acts that she considers objectionable. For our purposes, the most important question raised in *Smith* concerns whether the Court meant its holding to apply to the case of the student conscientious objector as well as to the case of the person who seeks to use drugs as part of her religious practice.

### *Does* Smith *Apply Only When Prohibitions Are Involved?*

To the extent that the Court in *Smith* held that the state could apply its criminal laws to *everyone*, irrespective of religion, the Court did not really "change" first amendment law. As mentioned above, many courts (such as the Oregon court in *Smith*) applied the compelling state interest/least restrictive alternative test *every time* someone made a free exercise claim. Other courts, however, applied this stringent test only when the claim was that the state was conditioning a benefit upon conduct proscribed by religion, such as when the state denies unemployment benefits to the Orthodox Jew who simply cannot work on Saturday. So, in a sense, *Smith* merely clarified the confusion in the lower federal courts and the state courts.

Moreover, the Court's approach in *Smith* makes some sense. There are many instances in which people could claim that their religions required them to be exempted from every conceivable type of law: criminal laws, laws requiring the payment of taxes, minimum wage laws, child protection laws, animal cruelty laws, etc. If the state had the burden to demonstrate a compelling state interest/least restrictive alternative every time someone wanted to "break the law" in the name of religion, then courts would be faced with the daunting task of determining which exemptions were justified and which were not.

The problem is that *Smith* leaves open to some degree the question of whether the Court was suggesting that the first amendment was irrelevant only when someone seeks an exemption from an otherwise valid *criminal prohibition*, such as in *Smith* itself, or whether the first amendment is also irrelevant *when the state conditions receipt of a benefit on conduct that is proscribed by a religion*, such as when a student objects to vivisection/dissection on first amendment grounds.

The lower federal courts and the state courts have, indeed, begun to extend the Supreme Court's decision in *Smith* to the civil context, from the criminal context in which it was decided.

The Second,[69] Third,[70] and Sixth[71] Circuits have explicitly rejected any civil/criminal distinction in the applicability of *Smith* in free exercise challenges to state statutes, and language used by other courts which have not yet applied *Smith*, indicates inclinations to abolish the traditional "compelling state interest" test for religion-neutral civil statutes.

The lower courts appear to agree on two exceptions to the relaxed *Smith* standard: (1) laws which directly regulate religious beliefs or religious-based conduct; and (2) "hybrid" situations in

---

[69] *Rector of St. Bartholemew's Church v. City of New York*, 914 F.2d 348 (2d Cir. 1990) (holding that an individual was not relieved of an obligation to comply with a "valid and neutral law of general applicability" under the free exercise clause (quoting *Smith*)), *cert. denied*, 111 S. Ct. 1103 (1991).

[70] *Salvation Army v. Department of Community Affairs*, 919 F.2d 183 (3d Cir. 1990) (extending *Smith* to the civil context concerning an exemption from the requirements of the New Jersey Rooming and Boarding House Act of 1979).

[71] *Vandiver v. Board of Educ.*, 925 F.2d 927 (6th Cir. 1991).

which laws violate the free exercise clause and some other constitutional right such as freedom of speech or freedom of the press.

Moreover, the Sixth Circuit has envisioned another situation where free exercise challenges may be raised under *Smith*. In *Vandiver v. Board of Educ.*, 925 F.2d 927 (6th Cir. 1991), a student sought to compel a public school to award him academic credit for course work completed in a religious home study program, when state law allows the public school to require students to pass examinations for courses studied at home. The court found that the regulation was a valid and neutral law of general applicability. The student did not have a religious objection to testing in general, but only to the equivalency testing requirement. The case did not, therefore, fall within the *Smith* exception for "hybrid" statutes which affect not only religiously-motivated actions but which also burden other constitutionally-protected rights, here for example, the right of parents to determine how their children should be raised. Without this "hybrid" quality, strict scrutiny remained the standard applicable to this situation.

The court noted, however, that "*Smith* does appear to leave open a small crack for free exercise challenges to generally applicable, religion-neutral laws even when such challenges are *not* joined with an alleged infringement of another constitutional interest."[72] The crack is found in the Supreme Court's statement that "[w]here the State has in place a system of individual exemptions, it may not refuse to extend that system to causes of 'religious hardship' without compelling reason."[73]

If the Supreme Court meant *Smith* to be read broadly, then *Smith* would alter the framework of analysis that would apply to student rights claims. That is not to say that student rights would no longer be protected, but only that the analysis described in section I of this chapter will not be able to be applied "automatically" to a student rights claim, and that protection of student rights will become more difficult. In order to understand the possible impact of *Smith*, it is necessary to understand the dis-

---

[72] *Id.* at 933 (emphasis added).
[73] *Id.*

tinction between free exercise claims involving exemptions from prohibitions, and free exercise claims, such as student rights claims, that involve conditions placed on the receipt of a state benefit.

Consider the following example: Joe practices a religion that requires him to run naked through the streets shouting obscenities. The state has a law prohibiting such conduct. This situation is analogous to the one involved in *Smith*, and under *Smith*, it would appear that the state can punish this conduct without the need to satisfy the compelling state interest/least restrictive alternative test, or, indeed, any other first amendment test. The first amendment simply ceases to be an issue in such cases.

Now consider a situation where Jane, who is an orthodox Jew, is fired from her job because she refuses to work on Saturday. This situation is very similar to the one in which a student is denied a state benefit—education—because she refuses to engage in vivisection/dissection.

Although the Court was not entirely clear, it seemed to recognize the difference between the two situations now under discussion. That is, the Court did not enthusiastically reaffirm the notion that the compelling state interest/least restrictive alternative test still had to be applied when the state conditioned a benefit on conduct proscribed by religion, but the Court did recognize that such a situation did require an analysis different from the one that applied to free exercise claims challenging the application of a generally applicable criminal law.

There are good reasons for distinguishing between the two situations described above. When a state provides benefits, such as welfare or education, the state generally has in place a system of individualized exemptions and exceptions. That is, the regulations, requirements and various criteria involved in such programs do not, unlike the proscriptions of criminal law, apply "across the board" without exception. Rather, such programs usually are more flexible and permit bureaucrats far more discretion in distributing those benefits. Because there is a greater possibility of discriminating against religion under such circumstances, it makes sense to say that the state cannot refuse to accommodate religious "hardship" without meeting the compelling state interest/least restrictive alternative standard.

For example, assume that a state university has certain requirements for a particular major, but, like all universities, has great
latitude to waive or substitute for such requirements. To the
extent that the university does have the ability to grant exemptions to students—and all universities do have such power that
they exercise regularly—the university should not be permitted to
deny an exemption to someone who requests one on religious
grounds without satisfying the compelling state interest/least
restrictive alternative test. To the extent that the state is not
required to meet the stringent test, then the chances are increased
that the university will deny an exemption to the student who
asks for one on religious grounds, *because* the university is not
acting neutrally, and is discriminating against the student *because*
of her religious beliefs. This situation is very different from the one
in which the state punishes those who are caught using narcotics
*irrespective* of the reason for the narcotics use.

It remains to be seen, however, whether the Court will, in
future cases, extend *Smith* to apply to *all* free exercise claims,
including the "benefits" situation described above. If the Court
does apply *Smith* across the board, then the protection of student
rights under the first amendment will be made more difficult, but
by no means impossible. To the extent that a student's claim
rests upon the first amendment, it will be necessary for the student to invoke one of two doctrines. We will discuss these doctrines below.

*Discrimination Against Religion*

If a student can show that the state is discriminating against
her *because* of her religious views, then she can prevail *irrespective* of whether the Court extends *Smith* to cover free exercise
claims in the context of state-provided benefits. That is, even
if the Supreme Court holds in a future case that the provision of
state benefits may be conditioned on conduct inimical to
religious beliefs as long as that conduct is required of *every* benefit recipient, a student who can show that the state is requiring the conduct in a particular case *because* the state is hostile

to her religious views can still win her case.

Consider the following example, which is a more specific application of one of the examples discussed above. Jane is a student in an introductory biology class at a state university. The instructor requires all students to dissect an animal, and Jane objects to this on religious grounds. She requests an exemption, and is refused—even though the instructor has granted exemptions to others who were unable to attend the lab for other reasons, such as illness or failure of transportation.

Under the law as it is currently applied, the state would have to satisfy the compelling state interest/least restrictive alternative test in order to impose the requirement on Jane. The state would argue that it has a compelling interest in setting its own educational requirements but Jane would, of course, point to the other students who were excused from the dissection requirement for other reasons as proof that the state does not really have a compelling interest. In such a case, a court would in all probability agree with Jane. The court would not have to find that the instructor denied Jane the exemption because she was discriminating against Jane's religious beliefs, but only that the state had failed to prove that it had a compelling interest in the dissection requirement.

If the Supreme Court were to apply *Smith* to such a situation, and hold that the state could require dissection by a student as long as it required dissection by *all* students, then the student would *still* be able to argue that the state was discriminating against her, precisely because it allowed others to have exemptions. The only difference would be that the student would have the burden to prove that the state was discriminating against her because of her religious beliefs. Under the current system, the state has the burden to satisfy the compelling state interest/least restrictive alternative test. This is not to say that the difference is insignificant: under current law, it is very difficult for the state to meet the burden of satisfying the compelling state interest/least restrictive alternative approach. On the other hand, however, it would not be particularly difficult for the student to carry her burden to show actual discrimination against her on the grounds of her religion.

## The "Hybrid" Nature of Student Objections
## to Vivisection/Dissection

In *Smith*, the Supreme Court did discuss a series of cases in which free exercise claims were coupled with other constitutional claims. In such "hybrid" cases, the Court in *Smith* recognized that the compelling state interest/least restrictive alternative test would still be applicable. For example, in *Wooley v. Maynard*, the Court held that a person may not be forced to display a license plate slogan that violates the person's religious beliefs.[74] According to the Court in *Smith*, the free exercise claim (that the person's religion was offended by the display of a particular slogan printed on the license plate) was also related to speech. That is, by requiring the person to display the slogan, the state was, in effect, making the person engage in *speech* with which the person disagreed.

Similarly, the Court in *Smith* pointed to its earlier decision in *Wisconsin v. Yoder*,[75] in which the Court had invalidated compulsory school attendance requirements as applied to Amish children. The Court in *Smith* also saw *Yoder* as a "hybrid" case because there the free exercise claim (that the state could not compel the Amish to attend secular schools) was coupled with a claim, recognized earlier by the Court, that parents had a constitutionally protected right to direct their children's education.

In at least two important ways, student rights cases brought under the first amendment do enjoy this "hybrid" quality—that is, they involve more than a free exercise claim alone. *First*, student objections to vivisection/dissection are frequently made by students who are active in various animal rights groups, or who, at least, are vocal in their expression of animal rights concerns. The denial of an exemption to such a student may be seen as an infringement not only of the student's right of religious freedom, but also of her free speech rights as well. Those who support vivisection/dissection are often very adamant in their hostility even to the expression of the idea of animal rights. To the extent

---

[74] 430 U.S. 705 (1977).
[75] 406 U.S. 205 (1972).

48

that the student can demonstrate that the instructor or her colleagues are hostile to the expression of animal rights ideas, then it may be argued that the denial of the exemption represents an attempt to stifle free speech as well as religious freedom.

*Second*, the Supreme Court has long recognized that parents should have some say in their children's education.[76] If a parent supports a student's objection to vivisection or dissection, then the additional parental right is triggered along with the student right. This may make the case a "hybrid" one that even the Court in *Smith* would recognize as governed by the compelling state interest/least restrictive alternative test.

### III. In Conclusion:

• The first amendment to the United States Constitution (along with similar provisions in state constitutions) protects freedom of religion.

• In order to qualify as a "religion," it is *not* necessary that the belief system be a traditional or recognized religion.

• In order to qualify as a "religion" it is not necessary that your belief system be theistic, *i.e.*, involving a God or Gods. It is sufficient if your belief system plays the same role in your life as would the traditional concept of God, *i.e.*, that your religion addresses some "ultimate concern."

• In order to qualify as a "religious belief," it is not necessary that a belief in animal rights (or anything else) be a formally recognized one within the total belief system; as long as you are sincere in maintaining your belief, and sincere in regarding your belief as part of your "religion," it is not necessary that others who share your religion also share the particular belief or recognize it as a belief that forms part of the religion.

• The first amendment absolutely prohibits the state from regulating your freedom to *believe* what you wish.

• The state may regulate conduct undertaken in the name of religion, but may do so only if the state can carry the heavy

---

[76] *See, e.g.*, Yoder, 406 U.S. 205 (1972).

burden to show that it has a compelling interest in regulating your conduct, and that there is no other way for the state to satisfy that interest while imposing a lesser restriction on your religious freedom.

• In *Smith*, the Supreme Court held that it was not necessary for the state to satisfy the compelling state interest/least restrictive alternative test when the state is seeking to apply a neutral criminal prohibition uniformly to all people. It is not clear whether the Supreme Court in *Smith* meant to eliminate the compelling state interest/least restrictive alternative test for *all* first amendment claims, including those, like student rights claims, where the state seeks to condition the granting of a benefit on the recipient's engaging in conduct that violates her religious beliefs. It is not likely that the Court meant to abolish first amendment protection for such situations.

• Even if the Supreme Court were to eliminate the compelling state interest/least restrictive alternative test for most first amendment claims, a student could still prevail if she could show that a vivisection/dissection requirement was being imposed on her and not others and that she was, therefore, being discriminated against *because* of her religious beliefs.

• Finally, the Court in *Smith* explicitly recognized protection for free exercise claims that are combined with other constitutional claims, such as the right of free expression or the right of parents to direct their children's education.


An Important Postscript:

The range of alternatives to the use of animals in the classroom is expanding rapidly. There are computer programs, models, diagrams, etc., and these alternatives are designed to fulfill the different pedagogical requirements of different educational contexts (*i.e.*, grammar school, high school, college, professional school, etc.). You should be sure to ascertain what alternatives are available early in the process of raising your objection. This information is available through various groups.

50

In recent years, the issue of conscientious objection to vivisection and dissection has frequently been in the news.

# 3
# Other Relevant Doctrines of Federal Law

## I. Additional Doctrines of Federal Law That May Protect a Student Who Opposes Vivisection/Dissection in the Classroom

In Chapters 1 and 2, we introduced and then discussed the primary source of protection for students who object to vivisection/dissection—the free exercise clause of the first amendment. In the vast majority of cases, the free exercise clause will be the primary legal concept upon which a student will rely. This is not to say that there are not other federal doctrines that may be used by students, usually in addition to the free exercise clause. These other doctrines are mentioned only briefly because if the student does not have a viable free exercise claim, these other doctrines will probably be of limited utility.[1] That is, although imposing a vivisection/dissection requirement on a student may also violate

---

[1] This is, of course, not to say that these other constitutional rights are not very important in other contexts insofar as the student animal advocate is concerned. That is, if the student is prohibited from wearing a button with an animal rights slogan, the relevant right would be found in the first amendment's guarantee of free speech. If students are prohibited from having meetings of their animal rights group, the relevant right would be found in the first amendment's right of free association. Our observation about the limited utility of these other doctrines is restricted to the role that they can play when the right in question involves conscientious objection to vivisection/dissection.

the student's free speech or free association rights, the primary right that will be violated in most instances will be the free exercise rights. Keep in mind that these doctrines also require state action.

*First Amendment: Free Speech & Free Association*

The first amendment not only guarantees to students freedom of religion; it also guarantees freedom of speech, which prohibits the government from infringing the right to engage in speech or expressive conduct,[2] and freedom of association, which guarantees the right to associate with others to pursue a common goal, such as the protection of nonhumans from exploitation.[3]

Often, school officials will retaliate against students who express pro-animal views or who are known to be allied with the animal rights movement. For example, one of our student clients made an announcement to her biology class concerning conscientious objection to a dissection requirement. The instructor subsequently denied that student *any* alternative, and made it known that she was very displeased that the student had made an announcement to the class. In this type of situation, the instructor has arguably violated the free speech rights of the student by deciding against an alternative at least in part on the ground that the student exercised her right of free speech.

In another case, a professor in a veterinary school said in response to a student's request for an alternative that the faculty would be unlikely to grant one because the student was a member of an animal rights organization that the professor considered to be "radical." Unfortunately (for the professor, that is), unrelated or otherwise unconnected people have the right to associate to pursue a common goal, and the professor may not violate the associational rights of the students.

---

[2] *See, e.g.*, Tinker v. Des Moines Independent School District, 393 U.S. 503 (1969).

[3] *See, e.g.*, Healy v. James, 408 U.S. 169 (1972).

54

In our opinion, the free speech and associational rights of students are almost invariably violated *whenever* school officials deny alternatives to students. The reason that the students' rights are violated is because the officials deny the alternatives *not* because the alternatives are not pedagogically sound, but because the officials are hostile to the students' animal rights beliefs, and because the officials seek to suppress animal rights speech within their institutions. In all of the student rights cases with which we have been involved thus far, we have discovered that the decision to deny an alternative has been based upon the decision of the faculty or administration to punish a student for the very expression of her animal rights beliefs, and because she was thought to be involved formally with one or more animal rights organizations. But students have a *right* to express their objection to animal exploitation and a *right* to associate with others who hold the same view. Consequently, in most, if not all cases, a claim of violation of speech and association rights is warranted.

## Due Process and Equal Protection

When the state violates an individual's substantive first amendment rights, it may also violate *another* constitutional right as well. Freedom of religion,[4] speech,[5] and association[6] are all "fundamental" rights. As such, whenever the state impermissibly places a burden on the exercise of one of these rights, there is actually another violation, *i.e.*, a violation of the due process clause of the fourteenth amendment, which forbids the state to deprive persons of "life, liberty or property without due process of law."[7] Deprivation of first amendment rights constitutes a deprivation of the liberty guaranteed under the due process

---

[4] *See, e.g.*, Cantwell v. Connecticut, 310 U.S. 296 (1940).
[5] *See, e.g.*, Gitlow v. New York, 268 U.S. 652 (1925).
[6] *See, e.g.*, N.A.A.C.P. v. Alabama, 357 U.S. 449 (1958).
[7] U.S. Const. amend. XIV, section 1.

clause, and the state's action must be analyzed under the strict scrutiny standard.[8]

Similarly, the equal protection clause of the fourteenth amendment prohibits discriminatory classifications based on the exercise of first amendment rights. That is, if a school does not give alternatives to those students with animal rights beliefs, such classification *itself* infringes the rights of free speech, free exercise, and free association. The state violates the first amendment rights *directly* by requiring a student to engage in an act (vivisection/dissection) that violates her religious beliefs, but the state *also* violates the student's equal protection rights by creating a classification based on the exercise of a fundamental right, which, in this case, is the first amendment right of free exercise. A classification that impinges on these rights triggers strict judicial scrutiny.

An equal protection claim is especially important when the school allows other students to avoid a requirement. For example, in one case in which we were involved, a particular surgery course which imposed a vivisection requirement was a prerequisite to certain electives essential to graduation from the college. The veterinary school gave failing grades to two students who refused to do the dissection required by the course. The veterinary school also denied these two students the opportunity to go on and take the cycle of electives because of their "F" grade in the "core" surgery course. *However, administrators did permit another student who had actually failed the surgery course*

---

[8] The "strict scrutiny" standard is one of two primary standards used by courts to evaluate constitutional challenges. The other primary standard is the "rational basis" standard. The standard that a court will use will depend on the right alleged to be infringed. If the right is considered a "fundamental" right, such as the first amendment right, then the burden of proof is placed on the *government* to show that the law satisfies a compelling interest in the least restrictive way possible. The court will apply "strict scrutiny" to the state's arguments. If the right is not a fundamental right, then the burden is placed on the person challenging the law, and the court applies the "rational basis" test under which the court will uphold the law *unless* the challenger can show that the state's law has no "rational basis." It is very difficult for a person challenging a state law to establish what is, in essence, the irrationality of that law.

*because of poor performance to continue with the upper-class electives.* A case of such differential treatment makes for a good equal protection claim.

In the above-mentioned contexts, the due process and equal protection guarantees are really secondary to the substantive first amendment rights. That is, if the school infringes a first amendment right, the infringement will generally be analyzed as a violation of a substantive first amendment right of free exercise (or speech or association) under the compelling state interest/least restrictive alternative framework discussed in Chapter 2. But such infringement will in all likelihood represent a violation of due process (because the liberty right is infringed) and equal protection (because of a classification based on the exercise of fundamental rights) *as well.* Accordingly, any lawsuit filed should probably mention due process and equal protection in addition to the substantive first amendment violation.

## Procedural Due Process

As mentioned above, the United States Constitution requires that governmental agencies treat all people in a fair manner. The fourteenth amendment states that the government may not "deprive any person of life, liberty or property without due process of law."[9] Accordingly, school officials may not impose punishment on students without first having followed certain procedures. How much process is due is determined on a case-by-case basis, but due process generally requires as a minimum that a student receive notice of the requirement and of her violation of the requirement, and a chance to be heard before being disciplined.[10] Since schools often threaten students who refuse to vivisect/dissect with expulsion, and since expulsion is a serious punishment, school officials must provide due process to the students.

---

[9] U.S. Const. amend. XIV, section 1.
[10] *See, e.g.,* Goss v. Lopez, 419 U.S. 565 (1975); Morrissey v. Brewer, 408 U.S. 471 (1972).

In most cases, the procedural due process issue will not be particularly significant. That is, if the school provides prior notice that vivisection/dissection is required, if the school provides notice to the student that the student is in violation of the requirement, and if the school allows the student some type of opportunity to be heard, then due process will probably be satisfied. If any of these elements is missing, however, then a procedural due process claim is warranted.

## II. Raising Federal Claims in a Federal Court: 42 U.S.C. Section 1983

*Introduction*

In Chapters 1 and 2, we introduced and then discussed the primary source of protection for students who object to vivisection/dissection—the free exercise clause of the first amendment of the United States Constitution. In the vast majority of cases, the free exercise clause will be the primary legal concept upon which a student will rely when objecting to vivisection/dissection in the classroom. In the first part of Chapter 3, we discussed briefly several other federal constitutional doctrines—due process, equal protection, and freedom of speech and association—that might also be used, either to supplement or to supplant the basic free exercise claim.

When a student sues in order to assert a claim under the federal Constitution, the student is, in essence, claiming that state actors are depriving the student of a right that is guaranteed under the Constitution. There is a federal statute—section 1983 of Title 42 of the United States Code, that allows the student to sue in *federal* court for such violations. In this section of Chapter 3, we will discuss briefly suits brought under section 1983. This discussion is somewhat technical, but the information is important to a complete understanding of the scope of relief available and also of the identity of possible defendants.

*Section 1983: Some Fundamentals*

In 1871, the United States Congress enacted the Ku Klux Klan Act, which read, in part, that "[e]very person who, under color of any statute, ordinance, regulation, custom, or usage, of any State or Territory, subjects [any] other person . . . to the deprivation of any rights, privileges, or immunities secured by the Constitution and laws, shall be liable to the party injured . . . . " This provision, which is now contained as section 1983 of Title 42 of the United States Code, was largely ignored because it was assumed to apply primarily to *officially* authorized misconduct. That is, if a person were deprived of a protected right by a state official acting under an officially authorized policy, or engaged in conduct that was so routine that it had become "custom or usage," then the affected person could bring an action under this section. If, however, the state actor deprived someone of her rights through an action that was *not* officially authorized or was *not* considered "custom or usage," then no action under section 1983 would be available.

In 1961, the Supreme Court revitalized section 1983 when, in *Monroe v. Pape*,[11] it held that actions brought under section 1983 were appropriate even when the police officers involved in that case had not acted in a way that was authorized by state law. Under section 1983, an injured party can get money *damages* against individual defendants who violate her civil rights, and she can also get an award of reasonable attorneys' fees, so as to provide an incentive to lawyers to take these cases in the public interest. Moreover, plaintiffs can get declaratory relief (a court declares that the plaintiff's rights have been violated) and injunctive relief (a court prevents the enjoined party from engaging in the conduct in the future).

This is not to say that there are no limits to liability under section 1983. There are, indeed, very substantial limits to this doctrine, and, as the judiciary becomes more politically conserva-

---

[11] 365 U.S. 167 (1961), *overruled* by Monell v. Department of Services, 436 U.S. 658 (1978).

59

tive, there are likely to be even more limits imposed on section 1983 relief.

The most important limitation on section 1983 actions is that although Congress did not specifically provide for immunity under section 1983, courts have held that certain forms of immunity for public officials were so established in the law that Congress could not have intended to abolish those immunities. These immunities apply to actions under section 1983 seeking *damages*, but, except in the case of legislators, do not apply to suits seeking *prospective* relief, such as an injunction or declaratory judgment. For example, judges and lawmakers enjoy absolute immunity from damages for actions taken within the scope of their judicial or legislative functions.[12] Prosecutors have absolute immunity for actions involved in prosecuting, but not in investigating, crimes.[13] Police enjoy a qualified immunity under section 1983 for actions undertaken with probable cause and in good faith.[14] Executive officials receive qualified immunity as determined by the scope of discretion and responsibility they possess.[15] In order to ensure that government officials are not unduly burdened by these suits, the Supreme Court has held that "government officials performing discretionary functions generally are shielded from liability for civil damages insofar as their conduct does not violate clearly established statutory or constitutional rights of which a reasonable person would have known."[16]

A *municipality* may be sued under section 1983 for acts that represent official custom or policy.[17] The Supreme Court has been unable, however, to articulate a test accepted by a majority of the

---

[12] Pierson v. Ray, 386 U.S. 547 (1967), *overruled* by Harlow v. Fitzgerald, 457 U.S. 800 (1982).

[13] Imbler v. Pachtman, 424 U.S. 409 (1976), *diverged from by* Harlow v. Fitzgerald, 457 U.S. 800 (1982).

[14] Anderson v. Creighton, 483 U.S. 635 (1987).

[15] Scheuer v. Rhodes, 416 U.S. 232 (1974). Please note that section 1983 is a *federal* statute that provides for relief against *state* officials. If a *federal* official is the violator of rights, then such an official may be liable in an action brought directly under the federal Constitution. In most cases, the same immunities apply.

[16] Harlow v. Fitzgerald, 457 U.S. 800, 818 (1982).

[17] Monell v. Department of Social Services, 436 U.S. 658 (1978).

Court to determine when an action constitutes official custom or policy.[18]

Until recently, unlike a municipality, the *state* and its officers acting in their official capacities, were *not* subject to a suit for *damages* in their individual capacities.[19] That is, if a state official was acting in her official capacity, then, unless the official was acting in bad faith, she could be sued for prospective relief (an injunction or declaration), but could not be sued for money damages. In November, 1991, the Supreme Court clarified the holding of *Will* and stated that a suit for damages could be brought in such instances.[20]

*Application to Cases Involving Vivisection/Dissection*

In most cases in which a student alleges that state actors have deprived her of her federally guaranteed rights (free exercise, freedom of speech or association, due process, or equal protection), there are a number of potential defendants. First, the student may seek to sue the school itself. Under section 1983, if the school is regarded as a "arm of the State," then a suit against the school *itself* would not be permitted under section 1983 because the State itself is immune from suit under the eleventh amendment to the United States Constitution.

In most cases, the student will seek to enjoin faculty members or administrators from entering a failing grade or dismissing the student, or seek declaratory relief consisting of a declaration by a federal court that the student's conscientious objection is protected by the first amendment or another constitutional provision or federal statute. In such a case, the student can seek relief against these state actors, but cannot seek money damages unless the particular state has waived its sovereign immunity.

If the student can show that the state actor (a faculty member or administrator for instance) "knew or reasonably should have

---

[18] *See* City of St. Louis v. Praprotnik, 485 U.S. 112 (1988); Pembaur v. Cincinnati, 475 U.S. 469 (1986).

[19] Will v. Michigan Dep't of State Police, 491 U.S. 58 (1989).

[20] Hafer v. Melo, 112 S. Ct. 358 (1991).

known that the action ... would violate the constitutional rights of the student affected, or if she took the action with the malicious intention to cause a deprivation of constitutional rights or other injury to the student," then the state actor can also be sued for damages under section 1983.[21] It is not enough merely to allege that the official acted with malice.[22] Rather, the student must first show that the official violated a clearly established right. The United States Supreme Court has yet to rule on the issue, but, for the reasons discussed in Chapters 1 and 2, the student's free exercise claim is very strong. In order to maximize the chances that a court will allow a student to proceed with a *damages* claim against state actors, a student (or her lawyer) should, in all correspondence with the school, indicate that the first amendment protects the student's conscientious objection, and that the institution has no basis upon which to deny the student's claim.

If the student has *concrete* evidence of malice, such as a statement by a professor or administrator that the student will be denied an alternative not because the alternative is not pedagogically sound but because the instructor disagrees with the student's animal rights *beliefs*, then the student may be able to overcome the bar against awarding damages against state officials.

---

[21] Wood v. Strickland, 420 U.S. 308, 322 (1975).
[22] Harlow v. Fitzgerald, 457 U.S. 800 (1982).

# 4

## Some State Law Doctrines
## That May Support a Student's Right
## to Refuse to Vivisect/Dissect

Up until now, we have focused exclusively on federal law doctrines that support the right of a student to refuse to vivisect/dissect. There are, however, five potential sources of further support to be found in state law.

*First*, state constitutions usually have provisions that are similar to the first amendment and that guarantee protection for the free exercise of religion, speech, and association. Sometimes, state courts interpret these guarantees as providing *more* protection than their federal Constitutional counterparts. That is, the federal Constitution provides for the *minimum* protection of civil rights and liberties; although the states cannot provide *less* protection than that required under the federal Constitution, states are free to provide *more* protection. For example, the New Jersey Supreme Court has interpreted the state constitutional guarantee of free expression to apply to a broader class of institutions than do the federal courts. Such an interpretation helps to overcome the "state action" requirement, and may allow a student to bring a challenge against the vivisection/dissection requirement of an institution that would be regarded as *private* (and hence, not a "state actor") under federal law.

The high courts of some states have interpreted their "free exercise" clauses to provide greater protection than the free exercise clause of the federal first amendment. For example, the Supreme Court of New Jersey has interpreted its free exercise clause to apply to at least some private actors.[1] Always research your state constitution to see whether the relevant first amendment guarantee is broader. If it is, then you have an additional constitutional safeguard. Even if the state does not provide broader protection, the state constitution must provide at least as much protection as the federal constitution and, accordingly, the state provision should probably be invoked in any lawsuit that is filed.

Reliance on state constitutional provisions will probably become more important as the Supreme Court interprets civil rights and civil liberties in more conservative ways.

*Second*, at least two states—California and Florida—have enacted legislation specifically designed to give students up to and including grade 12 the right to refuse to dissect. There are also efforts ongoing to get such legislation enacted in other states. For the text of the California and Florida statutes, see Appendix IV.

*Third*, some states have statutes that prohibit discrimination on the basis of religion in educational institutions. These statutes may apply to private institutions as well as public institutions. Again, always make sure that you research this issue under the law of your particular state.

*Fourth*, in most student rights controversies, the institution does its very best to make life uncomfortable for the conscientious objectors—even when the institution ultimately provides the alternative. Sometimes, faculty members and administrators will act in outrageous and hostile ways, and will encourage other students to try to alienate the "animal rights troublemakers." For example, in one case, professors at the institution openly criticized the students who protested vivisection, openly ridiculed the reverence for life philosophy of the animal rights movement, and refused even to investigate menacing behavior toward the objectors by other students who were also hostile to animal rights. In such cases, you are entitled to seek money damages on the

---

[1] *See* State v. Schmid, 84 N.J. 535, 423 A.2d 615 (1980), *appeal dismissed*, Princeton University v. Schmid, 455 U.S. 100 (1982).

ground that there has been an *intentional infliction of emotional distress*—a legal action under state law.

Whenever an alternative is denied for any reason related to the institution's hostility to animal rights, a tort[2] cause of action should be considered. That is, even if the student is never overtly harassed by instructors or others, the mere fact of denial of the alternative on the basis of hostility to animal rights may constitute tortious conduct.

*Fifth,* the denial of an alternative may represent a breach of the implied contract between the institution and the student. That is, an educational institution implicitly agrees that decisions affecting a particular student's education will be made only on the basis of what is pedagogically sound for the student and the institution. To the extent that an alternative is denied because the institution is hostile to animal rights, and *not* for pedagogical reasons, the institution has violated its implicit obligation to the student. Accordingly, when a student sues an institution and instructors for refusing to provide an alternative, the student should consider adding a cause of action based on breach of contract.

---

[2] The term *tort,* first mentioned on page 4, refers to a wrongful act, injury, or damage (not involving a breach of contract) for which a civil action can be brought.

A number of animal rights organizations have issued publications that not only question vivisection and dissection but promote and defend the concept of conscientious objection in the classroom.

# 5

## Asserting Your Rights:
## *Some Suggested Strategies*

*Know Thine Enemy*

In this chapter, we will discuss strategies that you should use in asserting your rights. All too often, people think that because they have rights, other people will respect those rights. Wrong, wrong, wrong. The history of humankind is one long, sad tale about people who regularly abuse others—humans and nonhumans alike. Indeed, many people think that they have the right to abuse others. You need to learn to deal with instructors and administrators who do not accept the notion that you have a right to object to the killing of nonhumans, and who think that they have the right to make you do whatever they tell you to do.

It is important to try to understand the mindset of those who are seeking to impose a vivisection/dissection requirement upon you. In many cases, these people will have different agendas, and, as in most other circumstances, thinking in stereotypes can be dangerous.

For example, most grammar school teachers and many high school teachers do not have any real personal investment in animal exploitation. As a rule, these teachers do not pursue research, do not have colleagues who do research, and do not work in institutions that depend heavily on grants from agencies such as the National Institutes of Health and the National Science Foundation. This is not to say that grammar school teachers and high school teachers will always agree to provide alternatives. On the contrary, in many cases, these teachers will be as adamant as any others. The difference, however, is that the less "invested" someone is in the institution of animal exploitation, the less she has at stake in the long run, and the more she will *generally* be willing to compromise.

Although grammar schools and high schools are slightly more flexible on the issue than are colleges, universities, and professional schools, there is a chance that they will become less flexible as the major science public relations groups, such as the American Medical Association, attempt to generate public hysteria about the animal rights issue. It is as yet unclear whether these groups plan to target grammar schools and high schools in their campaigns to "hold the line" against animal rights. For the time being, however, a wisely planned strategy by the student (and perhaps her parents), coupled with good, skillful negotiation, can in many cases result in a nonanimal alternative for a grammar school or high school student.

On the other hand, many instructors and administrators in colleges, universities, and professional schools generally have a very great stake in animal exploitation. Frequently, these instructors or their colleagues are involved in vivisection, and their institutions are heavily dependent upon federal grants for projects that use nonhumans. When a student asks for an alternative in such circumstances, many instructors and administrators do not even see the issue as one involving the student's rights under federal or state law or as one involving basic principles of respect for the views of others. Rather, the student is often viewed as an animal rights "fanatic" who is nothing more than a front for the movement. Once the student is seen as representing the *issue* of animal rights, instructors and administrators often conclude that they *cannot* grant an exemption without validating the student's belief in animal rights. Their perception is that such validation would threaten to undermine the entire industry of animal exploitation in science.

It should come as no surprise that the institutions most vehemently opposed to alternatives are veterinary schools. The reason for this opposition is clear. Despite public misperceptions to the contrary, veterinary schools are bastions for vivisection and other forms of animal exploitation. Many of those who are employed in veterinary schools have a vested interest in animal exploitation, and depend heavily on such exploitation as an important means of revenue. The veterinary establishment obviously has much to fear from the animal rights movement and, consequently, is committed to maintaining species discrimination, even in its most objectionable forms. To varying degrees, the same observations are valid for colleges, universities, and medical schools.

## To Sue or Not to Sue?

Many people think that as soon as they encounter resistance from an instructor or administrator, they should bring a lawsuit. Although lawsuits are sometimes necessary, they should be viewed as the tactic of last resort. There are at least two reasons to avoid lawsuits if possible.

*First,* lawsuits are expensive. Unfortunately, there are very few good lawyers who will take on such cases on a *pro bono* (no charge) basis. Even if a student is lucky enough to find a sympathetic lawyer willing to work for free, or on a reduced-fee basis, the attorney will still have to charge for her out-of-pocket costs, such as filing fees, fees for court reporters for depositions (oral examinations done before trial), fees for transcripts, and fees for expert witnesses. These costs can be very high. On occasion, animal rights groups will finance litigation, but the resources of the movement are nothing when compared with the resources of animal exploiters.

*Second,* lawsuits are time consuming. A lawsuit has a peculiar way of becoming a full-time job for all involved. This is not to say that the time is not well spent—some of the most important gains we have realized in the animal rights movement have come about as the result of litigation and other legal maneuvers. But lawsuits are a waste of time when you can get what you want without them.

Sometimes, however, lawsuits are necessary, and when they are, they should be pursued and pursued very aggressively. Although there are exceptions to every rule, animal exploiters usually have more to lose in public battles. Exposure is without any doubt the greatest threat to the exploitation of animals in the laboratory and classroom, and lawsuits are excellent vehicles for such exposure. Activists must not be afraid of legal actions, but should avoid the expense and delay involved if possible.

*What to do Before You Sue*

What follows is a series of steps (see Table 2) to pursue before considering litigation. We developed an earlier version of these steps several years ago and first presented them in an abbreviated form in the September 1986 issue of *The Animals' Agenda.* They have proved to be successful in many instances. In addition, even if you are not successful in resolving your dispute and need to pursue litigation, careful attention to these steps will ensure that you have an excellent record to bring to court.

Keep in mind that every situation is different and calls for a different strategy. These eight steps are intended to be used in a situation where, at least as far as can be determined, the teacher/professor is open-minded and has not already formed a negative view. If the situation is different, *i.e.,* if you know that the instructor is hostile to the animal rights movement and has always refused to offer alternatives, then you may want to dispense with any personal conversations with the instructor and rely exclusively on written communication.

**Step One:**
**Know yourself and how far you are prepared to go to assert your right not to vivisect/dissect.**

Fighting for your principles is never easy. Whenever you seek to challenge established institutions, you will likely encounter resistance. This resistance takes myriad forms—harassment by instructors and classmates, threats and intimidation, retaliation, and more. We have represented students in colleges and professional schools who have received anonymous threats and who have had teachers harass them in very subtle ways. If a lawsuit is

70

TABLE 2

# Before Litigation: Eight Important Steps

If you are not successful in resolving your dispute and need to pursue litigation, careful attention to these eight steps will ensure that you have an excellent record to bring to court.

**1.** Know yourself and how far you are prepared to go to assert your right not to vivisect/dissect.

**2.** Raise your objection at the earliest possible time, which should usually be as soon as you become aware that a course that you are taking or planning to take has a vivisection/dissection requirement.

**3.** Approach your teacher or professor alone or with like-minded classmates. State your objection to the vivisection/dissection requirement, and be prepared to discuss the reason for your objection.

**4.** Assess the situation carefully and intelligently.

**5.** Be prepared to present the instructor with one or more alternatives to the vivisection or dissection requirement.

**6.** Ask your teacher/professor to respond to your request promptly.

**7.** Document everything.

**8.** Seek legal help early and organize your support network.

required, there will be significant demands on your time and energy, and possibly, on your finances as well. If you are going to capitulate to these pressures, then you should probably not waste your time, or the time of other people.

You should have a clear idea in your own mind as to how far you are willing to go in challenging the institution. If necessary, would you be willing to discontinue your education—at least at that particular institution? Are you willing to have people regard you as a "trouble maker"? Questions such as these require some introspection, but those entering a situation like those under discussion must be prepared to reflect on these issues.

Moreover, you must be clear as to what *you* regard as a morally acceptable alternative *before* you begin. As discussed in Chapter 7, there are many different options presented as "alternatives." Some of these options do not require that the student dissect or vivisect nonhumans directly, but do necessitate the student's participating in an activity that indirectly involves the exploitation of a nonhuman. For example, watching a videotape in which an invasive procedure is performed on an animal is not the same thing as doing the actual procedure. It clearly does involve a more "passive" participation in animal exploitation; however, it may still represent a level of participation that is not acceptable to you.

If you raise an objection to a vivisection/dissection requirement and your instructor offers you a videotape alternative that you initially accept and then think better of later on, we can guarantee that your instructor will never let you forget that you initially agreed to a videotape alternative. You will be characterized as "wavering," "inconsistent," and "flakey," and your chances of getting a completely nonanimal alternative will be diminished. In addition, your opponents will use your change in position to support their argument that an educational institution simply cannot respond to the "shifting" preferences of students.


**Step Two:**
**Raise your objection at the earliest possible time, which should usually be as soon as you become aware that a course that you**

**are taking or planning to take has a vivisection/dissection requirement.**

All too often, students wait until the last minute before they make known their objection to a vivisection/dissection requirement. Any resistance that you are likely to encounter is merely increased if you first raise your objection two days before the vivisection/dissection is scheduled.

In addition, a delay in raising your objection will facilitate a denial by your opponents. If an instructor is able to say (even insincerely) that you would perhaps have been given an alternative if only you had raised your objection earlier, your position is weakened.

Finally, if you delay in raising your objection, you will have less time to seek support from sympathetic teachers and professors (who may occasionally have the courage to speak in your defense), classmates, animal rights groups, and other sources. Do not underestimate the importance of developing political support for your position.

**Step Three:**
**Approach your teacher or professor alone or with like-minded classmates. State your objection to the vivisection/dissection requirement, and be prepared to discuss the reasons for your objection.**

This step follows in part from the previous step. In raising your objection, try to do so in a context that will not put your teacher/professor on the spot and harden her in her opposition to your request for an alternative. It is generally not a good idea—at least in the first instance—to raise your objection to a vivisection/dissection requirement by delivering a speech to your instructor in front of 300 other students. Such an approach is substantially certain to create animosity. Approach your instructor alone or with some classmates who also object to the vivisection/dissection requirement. It is not a bad idea to have someone with you who will act as a witness to the conversation.

73

Inform your instructor that the vivisection/dissection requirement violates your religious beliefs and request an alternative. If your instructor asks you why you object, explain your concerns in a forthright way. There is no reason, however, for you to debate the issue with your instructor. As a student, you are not on equal footing with the teacher/professor, and she is well aware of that inequality and may attempt to exploit it by trying to intimidate you.

If your instructor refuses to give you an alternative, ask her why she is refusing. Make it clear that you believe that you are being discriminated against because of your religious principles. Follow up your conversation with a letter stating your understanding of the substance of the conversation.

Do not be confrontational in your initial contact with the teacher/professor. This is not to say that you should not be resolute in your position. Indeed, you should state your opposition to the vivisection/dissection requirement clearly and firmly. Make it clear to the instructor that you will not allow her to impose on you a requirement that violates your religious beliefs. Do not allow the instructor to goad you into shouting or otherwise losing your temper. If the instructor loses her temper, terminate the conversation and leave immediately. Keep records of the conversation, noting especially any threats or harassment by your instructor.

If you do not feel comfortable in approaching your instructor, or if you feel that she may later misrepresent the substance of your conversation, then you may decide to put everything in writing from the outset. Be aware that this has the effect of making your approach appear "legalistic" and may have a negative effect on some instructors and administrators. Nevertheless, there are situations in which putting all matters in writing is the best thing to do. This would certainly be the right tactic when the instructor or institution has a reputation for being hostile to animal rights concerns. In such a case, it is highly unlikely that the instructor is going to provide an alternative, and it is advisable to develop a good paper record from the outset, and to keep personal contact to a minimum.

**Step Four:**
**Assess the situation carefully and intelligently.**

Always try to learn as much as possible about your particular situation. For example, talk with classmates or more advanced students who have already taken the class in question to learn if the particular teacher/professor has taken a position on alternatives in past years. If you learn that the teacher/professor has denied alternatives in the past, you should assume that you will be denied as well. This is not to say that you should not approach the instructor personally or in writing concerning *your* objection, but only that you should be mindful that, in all likelihood, you are going to have to take further measures and you should plan accordingly.

Talk to classmates to try to determine whether students in other sections of the same course, or in different courses, have been given alternatives in the past. Speak to the instructors in these other courses to learn about the circumstances in which alternatives have been offered. Often, you will not be the first student with a moral objection to vivisection/dissection, especially if you are a student at a medical school or veterinary school. Many of the animal rights groups located around the nation maintain extensive records on these controversies and may be able to assist you in assessing the personalities involved in your particular situation.

When you speak to other students and instructors, you should exercise caution and discretion. Remember that whatever you say may come back to haunt you later.

**Step Five:**
**Be prepared to present the instructor with one or more alternatives to the vivisection or dissection requirement.**

To many instructors, the concept of alternatives is linked to the animal rights movement, and, therefore, they want nothing to do with alternatives. In one of our cases, a college biology professor refused to give an alternative to a student and wrote the student a letter stating that "[a]fter consultation with appropriate faculty committees . . . I [the professor] have concluded that there is no alternative work suitable to replace dissection in the laboratories."[1] The student brought a lawsuit, and during our examination of the professor, we asked her what alternatives she and her colleagues had considered and rejected. The professor replied that she and her colleagues had considered *no particular alternative.* Rather, they considered, and rejected, the "concept" of an alternative to the dissection requirement, and even though they had virtually no idea what alternatives were available, they decided that there were no alternatives.

The preceding account is not atypical. Most instructors are in a similar position with respect to their knowledge of alternatives. When you approach an instructor to ask for a nonanimal option, be prepared to discuss some specific alternatives. This requires that you do some homework beforehand, and that you educate yourself on the broad range of alternatives available for virtually all of the standard exercises that currently rely on nonhuman animals.

If your instructor rejects these alternatives, inquire as to her reasons for rejection, ask her to make those reasons clear to you, and take copious notes on the responses. In most cases, instructors will be unable to come up with any good reasons for rejecting an alternative. Indeed, their unsuccessful efforts to do so are often humorous. For example, in the case just discussed, we asked the instructor why she thought that a pictorial representation of a frog was not as good as seeing an actual dissected frog. The professor responded that the alternative did not provide the student with "proximity and sense of discovery." This is another way of saying: "The alternative is not acceptable because I say it is not acceptable"—and nothing more.

--------

[1] Letter from Barbara Bentley to Jennifer Routh, dated November 29, 1989.

## Step Six:
## Ask your teacher/professor to respond to your request promptly.

When a student objects to a vivisection/dissection requirement, an instructor will often say that she cannot respond to the student's request without thinking it over, consulting with colleagues, etc. Although the instructor may be acting in good faith, in our experience, this response is often a delay strategy on the part of the instructor and her colleagues, who have already determined that they are not going to offer alternatives. The instructor may then avoid giving a definitive answer until shortly before the particular lab in which the vivisection/dissection is to take place, and the student is left with little time to decide how to proceed. It is, therefore, very important for you to obtain a prompt response to your request.

If your instructor is noncommittal or negative, take your request to the appropriate supervisor, dean, or other administrator.

## Step Seven:
## Document everything.

It is very important that at all times you document your actions by keeping an accurate written record of dates, times, persons involved, and the substance of *all* conversations. Every time you speak to an instructor or administrator about your situation, take detailed notes on your conversations. If you write or receive a letter, keep copies in your files.

Again, remember to be *very* careful in what you say to instructors and administrators. It may come back to haunt you.

## Step Eight:
## Seek legal help early and organize your support network.

As soon as it is clear that your instructor will not respect your freedom of conscience and will refuse to offer an alternative, cease all personal contact with the teacher/professor and administrators concerning the issue and seek competent legal help. In addition, organize your support network. Contact other interested individuals in your class, school, or in the community who will help you to bring pressure on the institution. Demonstrations, if well-planned and attended, can be particularly effective in this regard. Other measures include letter writing campaigns and contact with political representatives. If you know prominent graduates of the particular institution, try to get them to exert pressure on administrators.

**Sample Letters**

The following is a series of sample letters that you may find useful in communicating with your teacher/professor. Remember, these are only samples and should not be used without first making whatever changes are necessary given your particular situation.

# Sample Letter #1

June 15, 1990

Dr. John Jones
State University of New Southland
Biology Lab
New Southland, Texas 22222

Dear Dr. Jones:

In the Fall Term 1990, I will begin my second year at the University of New Southland, and I have decided recently to declare my major as biology. Biology 103 is required of all majors, and you are listed as instructor for the course. I plan to take Biology 103 during this coming Fall Term.

In reviewing the description of Biology 103 contained in the catalogue, I have noticed that all students are required to participate in the dissection of a preserved fetal pig. I will be unable to participate in the dissection because of my sincerely held religious and moral beliefs about the sanctity of all life. Accordingly, I respectfully request that you provide me with an alternative to the requirement that will not involve my direct or indirect participation in the dissection of a nonhuman animal that has been killed for the purpose of classroom dissection.

I would appreciate hearing from you at your earliest convenience.

Sincerely,

## Note:

- The student is writing the letter on June 15—months before the course actually starts. As mentioned in Step 2, always approach the instructor at the earliest possible time. In this case, the student writes the letter soon after deciding to major in biology.
- In accordance with Step 6, the student asks for a prompt reply.
- The student indicates that she has a religious and moral objection but does not offer a detailed explanation. Do not volunteer more information than is necessary. If the teacher/professor wants more information about your beliefs, let her ask you for it.

June 15, 1990

Dr. John Jones
State University of New Southland
Biology Lab
New Southland, Texas 22222

Dear Dr. Jones:

In the Fall Term 1990, I will begin my second year at the University of New Southland, and I have decided recently to declare my major as biology. Biology 103 is required of all majors, and you are listed as instructor for the course. I plan to take Biology 103 during this coming Fall Term.

In reviewing the description of Biology 103 contained in the catalogue, I have noticed that all students are required to participate in the dissection of a preserved cat. I will be unable to participate in the dissection because of my sincerely held religious and moral beliefs about the sanctity of all life.

I understand from my discussion with other students that last year, you permitted several students who objected to the dissection requirement to use a computer model of a dissection. This same alternative would be acceptable to me, and I respectfully request that you provide me with this alternative.

I would appreciate hearing from you at your earliest convenience.

Sincerely,

## Note:

- The student has done her homework and found that Dr. Jones permitted an alternative in the past. The student indicates her knowledge of Dr. Jones's past practice (Step 4).

# Sample Letter #3

June 15, 1990

Dr. John Jones
State University of New Southland
Biology Lab
New Southland, Texas 22222

Dear Dr. Jones:

In the Fall Term 1990, I will begin my second year at the University of New Southland, and I have decided recently to declare my major as biology. Biology 103 is required of all majors, and you are listed as instructor for the course. I plan to take Biology 103 during this coming Fall Term.

In reviewing the description of Biology 103 contained in the catalogue, I have noticed that all students are required to participate in the dissection of a preserved fetal pig. I will be unable to participate in the dissection because of my sincerely held religious and moral beliefs about the sanctity of all life. I respectfully request that you provide me with an alternative that does not involve my direct or indirect participation in the dissection of a nonhuman animal that has been killed for classroom purposes.

As you may know, there are many alternatives to the use of nonhuman animals for educational purposes. For example, Carolina Biological Supply has available a plastic model of a fetal pig that has all anatomical features labeled and that includes a model key for reference purposes.

I would appreciate hearing from you at your earliest convenience.

Sincerely,

**Note:**
- The student mentions an alternative for consideration by the teacher/professor (Step 5).

81

# 6
## Selected Arguments and Responses

In this section, we wish to address six arguments frequently made by those opposed to granting students a right to object to vivisection or dissection. In most cases, those opposed are not really opposed to accommodating a student's religious or ethical beliefs—indeed, many of these critics routinely grant exceptions to accommodate students' religious beliefs. Rather, those who object to accommodating this *particular* belief (that it is wrong to kill nonhuman animals) are concerned primarily to frustrate anyone who is identified as being part of the animal rights movement. It is not unusual to find an instructor who will allow a student to miss a lab because the student is observing a religious holiday, but who will penalize another student who missed the *same* lab because that student objected to the vivisection or dissection involved.

In responding to objections raised by those who oppose granting a student a right to object to vivisection or dissection, you should first ascertain the general policy of granting exemptions from course requirements. If exemptions for reasons other than reverence for life are recognized, then the best approach to take is an assertive one: emphasize that you are being discriminated against because of your views and that you are being penalized when other students who are similarly situated are being accommodated. To the extent that the instructor tries to focus you on other arguments, keep returning to the point that the instructor's differential treatment is nothing more than discrimination against you based on the *content* of your belief.

As a second line of defense, you should not be reluctant to confront the substantive arguments that animal exploiters raise—in most cases, their arguments are not terribly sophisticated and may easily be rebutted. What follows is a description of these arguments, together with suggested responses.

*Objection:* If educators accommodate a student's conscientious objection to vivisection or dissection, then it will be impossible to limit the scope of the student right. Students with a broad range of beliefs will then be able to claim a right to be free from *any* requirement that supposedly violates these beliefs. For example, a student might object to taking calculus on the ground that it violates her "religion."

*Response:* Recognizing and accommodating a student's objection to vivisection or dissection will not facilitate challenges to *all* educational requirements. There is a world of difference between asking a student to *think* about something that she may find objectionable, and asking her to *engage in an action* that is inimical to her religious or moral beliefs.

For example, let us assume that a biology professor requires attendance at class sessions, and in one of the classes, expresses the view that the existing evidence supports the view that human beings evolved from other animals. In our view, the student would have a weak first amendment right to fail to attend class on the ground that she disagreed with the professor's viewpoint. If, however, the student were also required to make a statement before the class that she agreed with the professor's view, then, we think that the student would have a very strong first amendment right to refuse to do so.

Similarly, assume that the biology professor was lecturing about vivisection, and took the position that vivisection had provided benefits for human health. Again, we would find weak any claim that the first amendment protected the right of the student to miss the required class because the professor was saying something with which the student disagreed. The student's remedy would be to express her disagreement with the professor's position. But if the professor went on to require the student to engage in vivisection, then the student would have a right to refuse to perform an act that is inimical to her religious and moral beliefs. In sum, there is a clear difference between talking about something that someone might find morally objectionable, and forcing someone to do something that she finds objectionable.

*Objection:* A student who objects to a vivisection/dissection requirement is threatening the "academic freedom" of the instructor. That is, the principle of academic freedom protects the right of the instructor to teach that material and to impose those requirements that she feels appropriate.

*Response:* There are two responses to this argument. *First,* academic freedom does not provide absolute protection for what an instructor wants to do in the classroom. For example, an instructor is not free to engage in illegal conduct, such as racial discrimination or sexual harassment.

The limit of academic freedom is set by what is legal and what other instructors in the same discipline regard as legitimate. When vivisectors complain that animal rights activists threaten their academic freedom, they are simply begging the question. Activists are trying to get our society to recognize that vivisection and dissection are morally objectionable, and that the law should proscribe them. If activists win this battle, then there will simply be no right to exploit animals in the classroom. To say that such a victory by animal activists would violate academic freedom is like saying that the academic freedom of racists is violated when they cannot urge discriminatory treatment in the classroom.

*Second,* and more important, the student who objects to vivisection/dissection is not trying to stop the instructor from imposing the requirement on students who do not object. That is, although the student may believe that the instructor should not be able to use or to require the use of nonhumans at all, the posture of the argument made by the student under the first amendment is that the instructor cannot force that particular student to engage in conduct that is inimical to her religious and moral beliefs. The student is not challenging the right of the instructor to structure the course in the way that the instructor chooses— the student is only challenging the right of the instructor to violate the student's first amendment rights.

*Objection:* The conscientious objector knew that animals were used in the curriculum and took the course anyway, so she is bound to satisfy the requirement.

*Response:* If a student has a first amendment right to object, the fact that the student knew or should have known of a requirement is irrelevant for several reasons. *First,* the state cannot force a student to waive her constitutional rights as a condition of admission to the course or the institution. If the student has a right, she has a right, and her knowledge of a requirement that violates her right does not mean that she no longer has the right. Moreover, just because a catalog or course description states that animals are used in the curriculum does not mean that exceptions cannot be made, or that the stated policy was intended to apply to students with valid first amendment claims. Therefore, the presence of such a statement in a school catalog or course description would not even indicate to a student with a religious objection to animal exploitation that the policy applied to her.

In addition, it is common knowledge that academic institutions and individual instructors who engage in vivisection are often hostile to students with animal rights views. For example, at the University of Pennsylvania School of Veterinary Medicine, the admissions committee used to (and may still) ask prospective students whether they were sympathetic to animal rights, or whether they had objections to vivisection. If the student answered in the affirmative, she was not offered admission. In our view, such conduct on the part of a school is an outrageous violation of civil rights, and we can fully understand why a student would not feel bound by institutional statements that non-human animals are part of the course curriculum.

*Second,* a person's moral views often (and hopefully do) evolve. That is, a student may begin her career as, say, a veterinary student, without an animal rights orientation. She might then develop a commitment to animal rights during the course of her veterinary education. There is no reason why such a person should be precluded from raising an objection to a vivisection/dissection requirement.

*Objection:* The animal rights movement is a "terrorist" movement and, therefore, the student's objection is illegitimate.

*Response:* As moronic as this objection may seem, it is frequently voiced by those opposed to granting alternatives. The response is simple. Assuming that members of the animal rights movement do violate laws, such violations, even if amounting to "terrorism," have absolutely nothing to do with the student's religious belief. For example, the fact that Iraq invaded Kuwait has nothing to do with whether we should respect the right of a person to practice Islam. Similarly, even if some advocates of animal rights may engage in "violent" activities, such conduct has nothing to do with the constitutional protection that is afforded the free exercise of religion.

*Objection:* The student is not really a sincere conscientious objector because she is "inconsistent" in her views. She objects to vivisection/dissection, but [cats mcat], [wears leather], [hunts], [eats dairy products], etc.

*Response:* Those who invoke this argument seem to fail completely to understand the nature of protected belief. The whole point of religious freedom is that the student may subscribe to the views that *she* chooses, and not those that some vivisector chooses for her. As mentioned in Chapter 2, a court is free to inquire into the sincerity of a student's belief. In doing so, the court may determine that a student who objects to vivisection/dissection but who eats meat is not a sincere believer. Moreover, if the student does not subscribe to a theistic religion (*i.e.*, one focused on a God or Gods) and instead, subscribes to a "reverence for life" view, a court may have a difficult time concluding that the student really is expressing a protected religious view.

If, however, the court does determine that the student is expressing a religious belief (*i.e.*, is an adherent of traditional religious belief or otherwise holds a belief that addresses "an ultimate concern" of the believer), and is doing so sincerely, then the fact that the student may exploit animals in other ways should not have any relevance whatsoever. The student may sincerely—even if erroneously—believe that meat eating, hunting, etc., can be justified even given her religious and moral views about the vivisection/dissection requirement.

*Objection:* The student does not have to do the actual dissection, but need only [look at a videotape], [dissect an animal organ from a slaughterhouse], [look on while a lab partner does the actual vivisection/dissection].

*Response:* As discussed in Chapter 7, a student has the right to insist on a *nonanimal* alternative. That is, if the student adheres to the view that it is wrong to exploit animals for human benefit, then the student is entitled to an alternative that does not directly or indirectly involve animal exploitation. An animal killed in a slaughterhouse has been exploited and the use of that animal's body or body parts for vivisection/dissection purposes is an endorsement of such exploitation. An animal vivisected/dissected on videotape was itself the victim of human exploitation, and again, such an "alternative" is an endorsement of that exploitation. Watching your lab partner dissect or kill an animal might be morally preferable to doing it yourself in one sense—it presumably results in one fewer animal being exploited—but it is really no different from standing by and watching a friend commit an assault that you do not care to join.

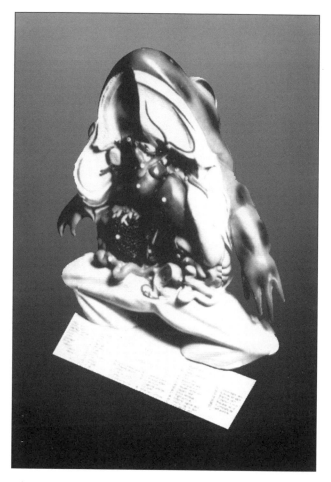

The increasing availability of non-animal options has strengthened the position of conscientious objectors seeking alternatives to vivisection and dissection.

# 7
# Nonanimal and Animal Alternatives

When a student seeks alternatives to vivisection/dissection requirements, she may be offered an alternative that does not require that she perform vivisection/dissection, but that does require that she participate directly or indirectly in some other form of animal exploitation. But the student must consider whether this is really an *alternative* or whether it also represents a morally unacceptable position.

For many—perhaps most—people who take the time to read this far, an alternative that involves animal exploitation is really no alternative at all. But we must nevertheless cover this topic for two reasons. *First*, students who request alternatives are often presented with options that do not *obviously* seem to be problematic, because they are, indeed, different from the vivisection/dissection requirement to which the student objects in the first place. In an apparent "flush" of victory, the student indicates her acceptance of the proffered alternative only to recognize hours or days later that she has basically agreed to something that she finds morally unacceptable.

Although in a perfect world the student should be able to return to her instructor and tell her that the proffered alternative is not acceptable and that the student requires a truly *nonanimal* alternative, we do not live in a perfect world. It is virtually certain that if a student changes her mind after accepting a supposed alternative, she will be met with all sorts of charges from faculty and

91

administrators that she is a "flake" and that her "vacillation" illustrates just how unstable and unpredictable she is. Should the case end up in court, the school will very likely argue that it cannot accommodate the student in part because she changes her mind all the time and, after all, how is an institution supposed to respond to a student who is not even sure of the nature of the religious beliefs she holds?

The student *must* reflect upon what type of alternative is acceptable *before* seeking an alternative. As recommended in Chapter 5, the student must think through the issue of how far she is willing to go—both as to whether she is prepared to litigate if the school does not allow an alternative, and as to what constitutes an acceptable alternative to her. Alternatives that represent other and different forms of animal exploitation are, not surprisingly, easier to obtain than alternatives that do not use animals or involve other forms of direct and indirect animal exploitation.

*Second*, a number of animal protection groups have been promoting animal-based alternatives in addition to nonanimal alternatives. That is, some organizations suggest videotapes of actual vivisection/dissection, or the dissection of animal parts obtained from slaughterhouses, as alternatives to vivisection/dissection. Such suggestions inevitably confuse students in their thinking about alternatives. After all, if an animal "rights" group promotes "alternatives" that involve exploitation, a student may nevertheless wonder whether alternatives that use animals should be acceptable to her own religious and moral views.

We are not suggesting that individuals or organizations that promote animal-based alternatives are *bad* in any sense. Indeed, if a student watches a videotape instead of performing the vivisection/dissection, she presumably decreases by one the number of animals who will be used for such purposes. However, watching a videotape of vivisection/dissection is, at another level, a completely inadequate alternative for those who really subscribe to an animal *rights* point of view. Watching a videotape of animal exploitation—and allowing a school to make you satisfy a requirement by watching animal exploitation on film—is very much the same as watching another student perform the vivisection/dissection, which, as discussed above, is a questionable "alternative." Moreover, many of these animal-based alternatives are obtained from companies that are notorious for animal exploitation in various contexts.

## What is An "Alternative?"

Strictly speaking, an alternative to a vivisection/dissection requirement is any option that will replace the requirement to which the student objects. In this broad sense, virtually *anything* can constitute an "alternative." For example, assume that a student objects to a requirement that she vivisect/dissect a dog. If the instructor offers her the opportunity to use a cat instead, the instructor has, in this very broad sense, offered an "alternative." But most people would regard such an "alternative" as ludicrous, unacceptable, and obviously offered in bad faith.

But what if the instructor offered instead that the student could use a *frog* instead of a dog? If the student's objection in the first place is based on her view that it is inimical to her religion that she participate in the killing or injury of *mammals*, then a frog may serve as an acceptable alternative. If, however, the objection is based on a broader concern that all sentient nonhumans have rights, then the vivisection/dissection of a frog, although different from that of a dog, is not an acceptable alternative.

The point here is simple: not all alternatives are equal! Just because an instructor may offer an "alternative" to a vivisection/dissection requirement, that does not mean that it is an acceptable one. The expression "alternative" is meaningless unless the student has a clear idea in her own mind about the *purpose* of her asking for an alternative.

## Nonanimal Alternatives

If the student takes the position that it is inimical to her religious views to exploit sentient animals by participating in their vivisection/dissection for educational purposes, then the student should insist—*and has the right to insist*—on a nonanimal alternative. In Chapter 2, we explained that courts are reluctant to engage in determinations concerning which religious view is the "correct" one. The fact that other students who object may be content with an alternative that still involves animal exploitation does not mean that those students and their views should set the standard for an "acceptable" alternative.

There are many, many truly nonanimal alternatives to vivisection/dissection for virtually every level of the educational process. These nonanimal alternatives include computer models, plastic models, etc.

We would argue that if a student adheres to an animal *rights* perspective, she should insist on a nonanimal alternative. There can be and are differences of belief concerning what rights nonhumans may have. Indeed, as a society, we are not even in agreement as to the extent of rights possessed by human animals. However, we do agree that if we are to talk meaningfully about human rights, there are certain rights that are so fundamental that they must be guaranteed. For example, it would not make much sense to talk about human rights if humans could be selected at random and tortured. Similarly, what force would the concept of rights have if humans could be selected at random and used in biomedical experiments?

If we believe that *nonhuman* animals have rights, it seems that we *must* be opposed to the notion that human benefit can always result in an abrogation of those rights. This is not, of course, to say that there might not be times when there are conflicts between the rights of humans and nonhumans. Indeed, there are often conflicts between humans who assert competing claims of right. Assume that, as a "joke," we yell "fire" in a crowded place, and our neighbor is trampled to death by hysterical people trying to escape the (nonexistent) danger. True, we have a right to free speech, but that right cannot be absolute, and must be balanced against other competing rights, such as the right of our neighbor to her bodily integrity.

Similarly, any right that a nonhuman has cannot be construed as absolute, and may have to yield to accommodate the rights of humans or other nonhumans in some situations. But if animals have at least some fundamental rights, those rights cannot be violated simply because humans may derive some benefit from that violation. We would, of course, argue that humans do not

94

derive *any* net benefit from *any* exploitation of nonhumans, because that exploitation inevitably threatens values that we consider most important to civilization: respect and compassion for *all* life and recognition that nonhumans do not exist for human "sacrifice" (whether on the altar of technology or at the dinner table). Moreover, we subscribe heavily to the notion that the use of animals in science does not advance progress but actually *retards* it.

If, however, the exploitation of nonhumans *did* generate benefit for humans, the mere existence of such benefit would not justify the exploitation of nonhumans and the violation of their rights. After all, it would invariably benefit some humans if they were permitted to exploit other humans. Our society does not permit this exploitation, however, *because* the concept of human rights acts as a barrier between those who seek to exploit and those whose exploitation would be beneficial to exploiters. If animals have any rights whatsoever, they must possess the right to be free from being regarded as the *property* of humans, and, accordingly, they must be protected from use as "teaching tools."

*An Animal "Alternative"*

Some animal advocates do not subscribe to a reverence for life philosophy or an animal *rights* perspective. This is not to say that these advocates are bad people, or that they have nothing useful to offer in the way of supporting progressive social change. For some advocates, an "alternative" to vivisection/dissection might well consist of using animal parts obtained from a slaughterhouse. For example, one animal welfare advocate suggests that a biology teacher who wants to provide an alternative may want "to get cow's eyes, intestines, brains, hearts, and other items from slaughterhouses."[1] Another pamphlet recommends as an alternative a videotape entitled, "The Frog Inside Out," which,

---

[1] Orlans, B., *Debating Dissection*, The Science Teacher (November 1988), at 39.

according to the pamphlet, "leads the viewer through an actual frog dissection."[2]

In a sense, these "alternatives" do accomplish an important function. To the extent that students dissect parts of animals slaughtered for food, or watch videotapes of animals who have already been dissected, they presumably cause fewer animal deaths in absolute terms. Although that advantage cannot be underestimated, the dissection of a cow's eye does strike us as absolutely *inconsistent* with the notion of animal rights. Similarly, watching a lab partner do what one refuses to do oneself may save another animal's life, but it still represents tacit approval by the student of notions that are fundamentally inconsistent with the idea of animal rights—that animals are "needed" as educational lab tools, and that it is acceptable for humans to exploit nonhumans.

_____

[2] Biology Methods Review Project, *Alternatives in Biology Education* 15 (A. Daniels, ed.).

# Conclusion

In this book, we have tried to explain the basic principles of a student's right to object to vivisection or dissection in the classroom. The primary thrust of our analysis has focused upon the free exercise clause of the first amendment, although it has touched on other federal and state law doctrines that support the student's right to object.

We emphasize—as we did at the outset—that this publication is not intended as a substitute for legal advice that takes into account the specific facts of any individual case or the specific legal doctrines that would be applicable to those facts. Rather, the purpose of the book has been to inform the student about some of her basic legal rights so that she can make a decision that is right for her. If a student decides to pursue matters legally, the first step is to consult an attorney.

The issue of a student's right to object is very important to the animal rights movement because in student rights cases, we see the intersection between issues of human rights—the civil right of a student to be free from state coercion—and the issue of animal rights—the student's belief that nonhumans should not be exploited for human benefit. It is imperative that we, as a movement, do everything we can to support those students who are courageous enough to stand up to a frequently oppressive system and to reject the exploitation of nonhumans.

# Appendix I

## Selected cases

*Africa v. Pennsylvania*, 662 F.2d 1025 (3d Cir. 1981), *cert. denied*, 456 U.S. 908 (1982)

*Ambach v. Norwick*, 441 U.S. 68 (1979)

*Anderson v. Creighton*, 483 U.S. 635 (1987)

*Blanton v. State University of New York*, 489 F.2d 377 (2d Cir. 1973)

*Blum v. Yaretsky*, 457 U.S. 991 (1982)

*Braden v. University of Pittsburgh*, 552 F.2d 948 (3d Cir. 1977)

*Burr v. Ambach*, 863 F.2d 1071 (2d Cir. 1988), *vacated sub nom. Sobol v. Burr*, 492 U.S. 902, *reaff'd on reconsideration*, 888 F.2d 258 (2d Cir. 1989)

*Burton v. Wilmington Parking Authority*, 365 U.S. 715 (1961)

*Callahan v. Woods*, 658 F.2d 679 (9th Cir. 1981), *on remand*, 559 F. Supp. 163 (N.D. Cal. 1982), *rev'd*, 736 F.2d 1269 (9th Cir. 1984)

*Cantwell v. Connecticut*, 310 U.S. 296 (1940)

*Chinea v. Benitez*, 702 F. Supp. 29 (D.P.R. 1988)

*Church of Scientology Flag Services Org., Inc. v. Clearwater*, 756 F. Supp. 1498 (M.D. Fla. 1991)

*Cohen v. President & Fellows of Harvard College*, 568 F. Supp. 658 (D. Mass. 1983), *aff'd*, 729 F.2d 59 (1st Cir.), *cert. denied*, 469 U.S. 874 (1984)

*Coleman v. Wagner College*, 429 F.2d 1120 (2d Cir. 1970)

*Cornerstone Bible Church v. Hastings*, 740 F. Supp. 654 (D. Minn. 1990)

*Damico v. California*, 389 U.S. 416 (1967)

*Davis v. Beason*, 133 U.S. 333 (1890), *overruled by Thomas v. Review Bd.*, 450 U.S. 707 (1981)

*Dettmer v. Landon*, 617 F. Supp. 592 (E.D. Va. 1985), *aff'd in part, vacated in part*, 799 F.2d 929 (4th Cir. 1986), *cert. denied*, 483 U.S. 1007 (1987)

*Eisen v. Eastman*, 421 F.2d 560 (2d Cir. 1969), *cert. denied*, 400 U.S. 841 (1970)

*Employment Div. v. Smith*, 494 U.S. 872 (1990)

*Frazee v. Illinois Department of Employment Sec.*, 489 U.S. 829 (1989)

*Gerena v. Puerto Rican Legal Services*, 697 F.2d 447 (1st Cir. 1983)

*Gitlow v. New York*, 268 U.S. 652 (1925)

*Goetz v. Ansell*, 477 F.2d 636 (2d Cir. 1973)

*Goss v. Lopez*, 419 U.S. 565 (1975)

*Grafton v. Brooklyn Law School*, 478 F.2d 1137 (2d Cir. 1973)

*Gregg B. v. Board of Educ.*, 535 F. Supp. 1333 (E.D.N.Y. 1982)

*Gresham v. Chambers*, 501 F.2d 687 (2d Cir. 1974)

*Hardwick v. Board of School Trustees*, 54 Cal. App. 696, 205 P. 49 (1921)

*Harlow v. Fitzgerald*, 457 U.S. 800 (1982)

*Healy v. James*, 408 U.S. 169 (1972)

*Heckler v. Ringer*, 466 U.S. 602 (1984)

*Hernandez v. Commissioner*, 490 U.S. 680 (1989)

*Hobbie v. Unemployment Appeals Comm'n*, 480 U.S. 136 (1987)

*Imbler v. Pachtman*, 424 U.S. 409 (1976)

*International Soc'y for Krishna Consciousness, Inc. v. Barber*, 650 F.2d 430 (2d Cir. 1981)

*Isaacs v. Board of Trustees*, 385 F. Supp. 473 (E.D. Pa. 1974)

*Jackson v. Metropolitan Edison Co.*, 419 U.S. 345 (1974)

*Jacques v. Hilton*, 569 F. Supp. 730 (D.N.J. 1983)

*John Birch Soc'y v. National Broadcasting Co.*, 377 F.2d 194 (2d Cir. 1967)

*Lewis v. Sobol*, 710 F. Supp. 506 (S.D.N.Y. 1989)

*McKart v. United States*, 395 U.S. 185 (1969)

*McNeese v. Board of Educ.*, 373 U.S. 668 (1963), *overruled by Fair Assessment in Real Estate Ass'n v. Neary*, 254 U.S. 100 (1981)

*Melanson v. Rantoul*, 421 F. Supp. 492 (D.R.I. 1976), *aff'd sub nom. Lamb v. Rantoul*, 561 F.2d 409 (1st Cir. 1977)

*Monell v. Department of Social Services*, 436 U.S. 658 (1978)

*Monroe v. Pape*, 365 U.S. 167 (1961), *overruled by Monell v. Department of Social Services*, 436 U.S. 658 (1978)

*Moose Lodge Number 107 v. Irvis*, 407 U.S. 163 (1972)

*Morrissey v. Brewer*, 408 U.S. 471 (1972)

*Mozert v. Hawkins County Board of Education*, 827 F.2d 1058 (6th Cir. 1987), *cert. denied*, 484 U.S. 1066 (1988)

*Naramuchi v. Board of Trustees*, 850 F.2d 70 (2d Cir. 1988)

*N.A.A.C.P. v. Alabama*, 357 U.S. 449 (1958)

*Patrick v. Le Fevre*, 745 F.2d 153 (2d Cir. 1984)

*Patsy v. Board of Regents*, 457 U.S. 496 (1982)

*Pembaur v. Cincinnati*, 475 U.S. 469 (1986)

*People v. Woody*, 61 Cal. 2d 716, 394 P.2d 813, 40 Cal. Rptr. 69 (1964)

*Pierson v. Ray*, 386 U.S. 547 (1967), *overruled by Harlow v. Fitzgerald*, 457 U.S. 800 (1982)

*Plano v. Baker*, 504 F.2d 595 (2d Cir. 1974)

*Public Utilities Comm'n v. Pollak*, 343 U.S. 451 (1952)

*Quackenbush v. Johnson City School Dist.*, 716 F.2d 141 (2d Cir. 1983)

*Quaring v. Peterson*, 720 F.2d 1121 (8th Cir. 1984), *aff'd sub nom. Jensen v. Quaring*, 472 U.S. 478 (1985)

*Rackin v. University of Pennsylvania*, 386 F. Supp. 992 (E.D. Pa. 1974)

*Rector of St. Bartholemew's Church v. City of New York*, 914 F.2d 348 (2d Cir. 1990), *cert. denied*, 111 S. Ct. 1103 (1991)

*Reitman v. Mulkey*, 387 U.S. 369 (1967)

*Rendell-Baker v. Kohn*, 457 U.S. 830 (1982)

*Reynolds v. United States*, 98 U.S. 145 (1879), *overruled by Thomas v. Review Bd.*, 450 U.S. 707 (1981)

*Riley v. Ambach*, 668 F.2d 635 (2d Cir. 1981)

*St. Louis v. Praprotnik*, 485 U.S. 112 (1988)

*Salvation Army v. Department of Community Affairs*, 919 F.2d 183 (3d Cir. 1990)

*Scheuer v. Rhodes*, 416 U.S. 232 (1974)

*Shelley v. Kraemer*, 334 U.S. 1 (1948)

*Sherbert v. Verner*, 374 U.S. 398 (1963)

*Siletti v. New York City Employees Retirement System*, 401 F. Supp. 162 (S.D.N.Y. 1975), *aff'd*, 556 F.2d 559 (2d Cir. 1977), *cert. denied*, 434 U.S. 829 (1977)

*Society of Separationists, Inc. v. Herman*, 939 F.2d 1207 (5th Cir. 1991)

*Spence v. Bailey*, 465 F.2d 797 (6th Cir. 1972)

*State v. Schmid*, 84 N.J. 535, 423 A.2d 615 (1980), *appeal dismissed, Princeton University v. Schmid*, 455 U.S. 100 (1982)

*Steffel v. Thompson*, 415 U.S. 452 (1974)

*Stevens v. Berger*, 428 F. Supp. 896 (E.D.N.Y. 1977)

*Thomas v. Review Board*, 450 U.S. 707 (1981)

*Tinker v. Des Moines Independent School District*, 393 U.S. 503 (1969)

*Torasco v. Watkins*, 367 U.S. 488 (1961)

*United States v. Ballard*, 322 U.S. 78 (1944)

*United States v. Kahane*, 396 F. Supp. 687 (E.D.N.Y.), *modified sub nom. Kahane v. Carlson*, 527 F.2d 492 (2d Cir. 1975)

*United States v. Kauten*, 133 F.2d 703 (2d Cir. 1943)

*United States v. Kuch*, 288 F. Supp. 439 (D.D.C. 1968)

*United States v. Lee*, 455 U.S. 252 (1982)

*United States v. Lewis*, 638 F. Supp. 573 (W.D.Mich. 1986)

# Appendix II

# Sample Legal Pleading

IN THE UNITED STATES DISTRICT COURT
FOR THE SOUTHERN DISTRICT OF OHIO
EASTERN DIVISION

---

JENNIFER KISSINGER,      :

     : 

     Plaintiff,      :

     :

v.      :      CIVIL ACTION

     :

THE BOARD OF TRUSTEES OF OHIO STATE      JURY DEMAND
UNIVERSITY-COLLEGE OF VETERINARY      :      ENDORSED HEREON
MEDICINE, RONALD WRIGHT, WILLIAM
MUIR, JAMES BLAKESLEE, LAWRENCE      :
HEIDER, RICHARD BEDNARSKI,      DOCKET NO. C2-90-887
STEPHEN J. BIRCHARD, in their      :
official capacities, and
MILTON WYMAN, in his official      :
capacity and individually,

     :

     Defendants.

---

## COMPLAINT

Plaintiff, Jennifer Kissinger, residing at 422 East 20th Ave., Apt. J, Columbus, Ohio, 43201, by way of Complaint against the Defendants named herein says:

## INTRODUCTION

1. This action is brought to enjoin Defendants from penalizing Plaintiff, a veterinary student who refuses on sincerely held religious and moral grounds to use and kill healthy animals as

105

part of her laboratory requirements, where alternatives acceptable to the student are available. Declaratory relief is also sought. In failing to respect Plaintiff's sincerely held religious and moral beliefs, Defendants are in violation of the protections granted her under the free exercise clause of the first amendment of the United States Constitution, and the analogous provision of the Ohio State Constitution. Defendants are also in violation of the free speech and free association protection granted her under the first amendment of the United States Constitution and the analogous provisions of the Ohio State Constitution. Defendants have further violated the due process guarantee afforded Plaintiff under the United States Constitution, and the equal protection guarantees afforded by the United States Constitution and analogous provisions of the Ohio State Constitution.

Additionally, Defendants have breached their contractual obligation to Plaintiff, and induced her to rely detrimentally on misleading assertions. Finally, Defendant Wyman has exhibited a reckless, wanton, and malicious disregard for Plaintiff's religious and moral beliefs and has caused emotional harm to Plaintiff.

## JURISDICTION

2. This action arises under the first amendment of the Constitution of the United States; the analogous provision of the Ohio State Constitution; and the Civil Rights Act, namely 42 U.S.C. § 1983. Jurisdiction is conferred on this Court by 28 U.S.C. § 1331 and 28 U.S.C. § 1343. Declaratory relief is sought under 28 U.S.C. §§ 2201 and 2202. Pendant claims under state law are also alleged.

3. No adequate administrative remedies are available that can provide the relief requested by Plaintiff.

## PARTIES

4. Plaintiff, Jennifer Kissinger, is a third year veterinary student at Ohio State University - College of Veterinary Medicine

("OSU-CVM") and resides at 422 East 20th Ave., Apt. 3, Columbus, Ohio, 43201.

5. Defendant Milton Wyman is named as a Defendant in this action, both as an individual and in his official capacity. To the best of Plaintiff's knowledge and belief, Defendant Wyman is an Associate Dean, Office of Student Affairs, and Dean of Students, at OSU-CVM. In his capacity as student advocate, Defendant Wyman is obligated to be available to all veterinary students for consultation regarding their professional program and personal problems. It is his designated responsibility to ensure that productive and meaningful lines of communications are maintained between students, faculty and administration and that students' problems are addressed in a meaningful manner.

6. Defendant Ronald Wright is named as a Defendant in this action, in his official capacity. To the best of Plaintiff's knowledge and belief, Defendant Wright is the Dean of OSU-CVM.

7. Defendant William Muir is named as a Defendant in this action, in his official capacity. To the best of Plaintiff's knowledge and belief, Defendant Muir is a Professor and Chairman of the Department of Veterinary Clinical Sciences at OSU-CVM.

8. Defendant James Blakeslee is named as a Defendant in this action, in his official capacity. To the best of Plaintiff's knowledge and belief, Defendant Blakeslee is the Chair of the Veterinary Anatomy Department at OSU-CVM.

9. Defendant Lawrence Heider is named as a Defendant in this action, in his official capacity. To the best of Plaintiff's knowledge and belief, Defendant Heider is the Chair of Preventative Medicine at OSU-CVM.

10. Defendant Richard Bednarski is named as a Defendant in this action, in his official capacity. To the best of Plaintiff's knowledge and belief, Defendant Bednarski is an Associate Professor and Head of the Anesthesiology Department of Veterinary Clinical Sciences at OSU-CVM.

11. Defendant Stephen J. Birchard is named as a Defendant in this action, in his official capacity. To the best of

Plaintiff's knowledge and belief, Defendant Birchard is an Associate Professor, Acting Team Leader of the Operative Practice (VM 620), and Head of the Small Animal Surgery Section, Department of Veterinary Clinical Sciences at OSU-CVM.

12. The Board of Trustees of the Ohio State University-School of Veterinary Medicine are a duly appointed Board of Trustees of a state educational institution, and as such are state actors for purposes of the United States Constitution. OSU-CVM has delegated its authority regarding curricular control and standards for passing and failing students to its faculty, and at all times relevant herein, the faculty's actions are pursuant to this delegated authority and are under color of state law.

**VENUE**

13. Venue is properly laid in this Court since all of the events leading to this cause of action occurred in Columbus, Ohio. As the claim arose here, 28 U.S.C. § 1391(a) permits that venue be laid in this District.

**STATEMENT OF FACTS**

14. Plaintiff is a third year veterinary student at OSU-CVM and is currently enrolled in the College's Operative Practice and Techniques Course 620/621 (hereinafter "course 620/21").

15. To the best of Plaintiff's knowledge and belief, course 620/21 is a required course designed to teach students to administer technical and surgical skills.

16. To the best of Plaintiff's knowledge and belief, course 620/21 is a prerequisite to other required courses.

17. Plaintiff has sincerely held religious and moral objections to the killing of healthy animals and the performance of surgical techniques on healthy animals solely for educational purposes when accepted alternatives exist. Her religious and moral beliefs relate to an ultimate concern and influence Plaintiff's life in a profound way, affecting, among other things, her diet, her choice of clothing, and her views about the use of animals in experiments and education.

108

18. Alternative curricula have been set up at several veterinary medical colleges across the United States, and abroad. These alternative curricula offer a range of options to students who conscientiously object to the killing of healthy animals and the performance of surgical techniques on healthy animals solely for educational purposes. Students who have learned by these alternative means have graduated and competed successfully for employment in the veterinary medical field.

19. OSU-CVM has already indicated that it accepts as pedagogically sound alternatives that are offered at other veterinary schools.

20. In or about January of 1990, Plaintiff notified the faculty of OSU-CVM of her objections to the course 620/21 curriculum and requested information regarding the availability of an alternative.

21. In or about the week of April 16, 1990, Plaintiff met with Dr. Smeak who informed her of a student participation spay/neuter clinic scheduled to be functional in the fall, when she would need to have an alternative, and suggested that, as an alternative, she learn the required surgery skills with an outside veterinarian, Dr. Deborah McMichael, with whom Plaintiff had previously worked.

22. In or about the week of April 16, 1990, Plaintiff met with Defendant Wyman, at which time Defendant Wyman said that he and most of the faculty disagreed with Plaintiff's position. He stated his fear that if an alternative were available for Plaintiff, other students might also want an alternative. He told Plaintiff that she could fulfill her surgery requirements at OSU-CVM by taking the alternative program offered at Tufts University Veterinary School, and then returning to OSU-CVM for her senior year.

23. On or about April 30, 1990, Dr. Smeak informed Plaintiff that the idea of working with a private veterinarian as an alternative would not be approved by OSU-CVM.

24. On or about May 1, 1990, Defendant Wyman told Plaintiff

that she probably would not have been admitted as a student at OSU-CVM if she had expressed her religious and moral views when she applied for admission.

25. On or about May 1, 1990, Plaintiff met with Defendant Birchard, at which time he informed Plaintiff that the faculty would discuss a proposal for an alternative in a meeting on May 8, 1990. Plaintiff asked to attend to present her views, but was told not to attend, since her opinions were of no importance. Upon information and belief, this meeting was held sometime in early May, but no final decision regarding an alternative was made at that time.

26. On or about June 14, 1990, Plaintiff met with Defendant Blakeslee, who asked about Plaintiff's involvement with the animal rights movement and stated a fear that those who believed in animal rights were infiltrating the campus and that the Plaintiff should not "make waves." Defendant Blakeslee told Plaintiff that it would be in her best interest to fulfill the OSU-CVM surgery requirement by taking the equivalent course at Tufts, since Tufts already had in place an alternative.

27. On or about June 15, 1990, Plaintiff met with Defendant Heider, who stated that his major objection to providing an alternative is that it would drain the school's resources, and take prime faculty members and administrators away from their duties.

28. On or about June 18, 1990, in a meeting with Dr. Smeak, Plaintiff was informed that although the surgery department had approved an alternative for Plaintiff, the faculty had met and rejected the implementation of an alternative and that the faculty was directed not to speak with Plaintiff.

29. In addition, on or about June 18, 1990, Defendant Muir told Plaintiff in an afternoon meeting that the faculty had rejected an alternatives proposal for three reasons: (1) an alternative would cost money; (2) it would occupy faculty members' time and detract from their other duties; and (3) an alternative entailing work on client-owned animals would interfere

110

with the education of seniors who would otherwise have handled those cases.

30. After continuing to meet with faculty and members of the administration for the purpose of finding an acceptable alternative, Defendant Wyman called Plaintiff in the morning of June 26, 1990 and informed her that she could present her concerns in a faculty meeting later that afternoon. After making a presentation and answering questions from the faculty, Plaintiff was asked to leave so that the faculty could deliberate over the alternatives issue.

31. In a letter from Defendant Wyman to Plaintiff, dated June 27, 1990, Defendant Wyman stated that Defendant Wright had formed an ad hoc college-wide committee to develop an alternative program for the use of animals in OSU-CVM teaching programs. Defendant Wyman stated that the development of the alternative might extend beyond fall quarter, necessitating possible modification in Plaintiff's educational timetable, and making it appear as if an alternative would be in place in a relatively timely fashion. Plaintiff indicated that this would be acceptable and acted in reliance on Defendant Wyman's representation.

32. In or about the week of July 2, 1990, Defendant Wyman stated that the committee was working on an alternative at that time, so that it would not be "unreasonable" to think that the committee might have the alternative developed by winter quarter, again making it appear as if an alternative would be in place in a relatively timely fashion. Again, Plaintiff indicated that this would be acceptable and acted in reliance on Defendant Wyman's representation

33. As a result of Defendant Wyman's June 27 letter and the subsequent meeting, Plaintiff reasonably believed that the faculty and administration were sensitive to her position and would accommodate her religious and moral convictions within a reasonable time.

34. During July 1990, Plaintiff met with Dr. David Wilkie, who is the chair of the OSU-CVM ad hoc committee on alternatives.

Dr. Wilkie stated that he was enthusiastic about developing an alternative, and discussed various specific types of alternatives with Plaintiff. As a result, Plaintiff reasonably believed that the faculty and administration were sensitive to her position and would accommodate her religious and moral convictions within a reasonable time.

35. In or about the end of August, 1990, Defendant Wyman indicated to Plaintiff for the first time that the committee might not ever institute an alternative. As a result, Plaintiff canceled her plans for a September internship with a veterinarian practicing in Maryland so that she could devote her time to trying to obtain an alternative.

36. By letter dated September 13, 1990, Defendants' Counsel, Gary E. Brown and James E. Meeks, stated that it was the judgment of the faculty of the College that it is impossible to properly train a veterinarian without using some live, acquired animals, that there is simply no way that Plaintiff can complete, now or in the foreseeable future, the 620/21 course sequence without performing the procedures that violate Plaintiff's sincerely held religious and moral beliefs, and that if she is unwilling to do these procedures she will fail the course. The letter further states that failure to perform the surgery will result in preclusion from ever earning a degree at OSU-CVM. The letter then states that if Plaintiff's beliefs are so strong on this issue, she should consider a different career path.

37. On September 19, 1990, Plaintiff began her fall quarter. Since that time, she has sought and received reading and other assignments by instructors in course 620/21. She has completed each assignment given to her and in every possible way has attempted to learn the information and skills necessary to her chosen profession.

38. On or about September 20, 1990, Ms. Betty Hudson, of the Provost's office, told Plaintiff that it would take at least four to five years to establish an alternative.

39. In a letter, dated September 21, 1990, Plaintiff was told

by Defendant Birchard, that failure to participate in the Operative Practice Laboratories without a valid excuse will result in a failing grade at the end of Fall Quarter.

40. In a letter from Defendant Bednarski, Head of Anesthesiology, dated September 26, 1990, Plaintiff was informed that it is the position of the anesthesia faculty that there currently exists no acceptable alternative to participation in the Operative Practice course, and that Plaintiff would receive a failing grade for all anesthesia laboratories.

41. In a letter from Defendant Muir, dated September 27, 1990, Plaintiff was informed that she has been issued a failing grade for the September 20, 1990 laboratory, in which she refused to participate for religious reasons.

42. On October 3, 1990, Defendant Wyman requested a meeting with Plaintiff. At this meeting, Defendant Wyman explained that he simply requested the meeting since procedure dictated that he meet with any "failing" student. Having fulfilled the protocol requirements for "failing" students, Defendant Wyman had nothing further to say and the meeting was concluded.

43. On or about November 7, 1990, certain OSU-CVM students circulated a letter that criticized Plaintiff, and that had been edited upon the advice of Defendant Wyman to exclude reference to Plaintiff's religious beliefs, further demonstrating Defendant Wyman's utter disregard for Plaintiff's free exercise of her religion.

44. On November 7, 1990, Defendant Wyman held a meeting of Plaintiff's class, ostensibly to discuss curricular concerns. At that meeting, Defendant Wyman ridiculed Plaintiff's religious and moral beliefs, misrepresented Plaintiff's position about her request for an alternative, and did nothing to stop other students in the room from ridiculing Plaintiff's religious and moral beliefs.

45. On November 16, 1990, Plaintiff participated in a radio interview on WTVN in Columbus, Ohio. The host of the interview was Mr. James Bleikamp. Also interviewed during the same program

were two of Plaintiff's fellow students, Mr. John Manolukas and Mr. George Belbey. During the interview, Mr. Manolukas admitted that he had received information about Plaintiff's request for an educational alternative from Defendant Wyman. Plaintiff maintains that the information provided by Defendant Wyman to Mr. Manolukas was viewed as confidential by Plaintiff and, in any event, was not represented accurately.

46. To the best of Plaintiff's knowledge and belief, at least one other student at OSU-CVM has continued to be enrolled in the veterinary school, as a senior, without having passed a junior level course.

47. To the best of Plaintiff's knowledge and belief, other students at OSU-CVM were allowed to perform many techniques on client-owned animals without having any prior experience in live acquired animal surgery and/or techniques.

48. To the best of Plaintiff's knowledge and belief, at least one other student has been provided with alternatives in senior-level mandatory courses at OSU-CVM.

49. Plaintiff has been and remains ready, willing, and able to perform alternative work in order to satisfy the requirements of course 620/21. She has proposed, as an alternative, that she participate in every aspect of course 620/21 that does not involve live animal use, that she practice surgical and technical skills on cadavers of animals that were not killed solely for educational purposes, that she perform surgery on client-owned or other non-experimental animals who require the procedures under the supervision of a veterinarian (and to receive an "incomplete" until such arrangements are made), that she extend her surgical rotations during her fourth year, and that she take all surgical electives offered to fourth-year students which utilize client-owned or other non-experimental animals, to ensure adequate experience in live animal surgery.

50. Plaintiff has suffered and is suffering the following harm: (1) Plaintiff has received and will continue to receive zero credit towards her third year surgery lab requirements as a

114

result of her religious and moral beliefs; (2) Plaintiff is facing imminent failure of required course 620/21; (3) Plaintiff is facing imminent expulsion from school by mid-December 1990; and (4) Defendants' discriminatory actions have threatened Plaintiff's career and wasted valuable time and resources.

## COUNT ONE

51. Plaintiff repeats each and every allegation contained in paragraphs 1 through 49, as set forth herein in their entirety and makes the same a part hereof by reference thereto.

52. Defendants' refusal to provide Plaintiff an alternative, despite Plaintiff's sincerely held religious and moral beliefs, deny Plaintiff the right to free exercise of religion under the first amendment of the Constitution of the United States, as applied to the State of Ohio by the fourteenth amendment to the Constitution of the United States. In addition, Defendants' actions and policies undertaken pursuant to the laws, customs, usages, and practices of the State of Ohio are, therefore, unconstitutional and unlawful pursuant to 42 U.S.C. § 1983.

## COUNT TWO

53. Plaintiff repeats each and every allegation contained in paragraphs 1 through 51, as set forth herein in their entirety and makes the same a part hereof by reference thereto.

54. Defendants' refusal to provide Plaintiff an alternative, despite Plaintiff's sincerely held religious and moral beliefs, violate Article I, section 7 of the Ohio State Constitution, which guarantees inalienable rights including the free exercise of
religion.

## COUNT THREE

55. Plaintiff repeats and realleges the allegations of paragraphs 1 through 53, as set forth herein in their entirety and makes the same a part hereof by reference thereto.

56. Defendants' actions, including, but not limited to,

115

inquiring into Plaintiff's animal rights beliefs, instructing Plaintiff not to "make waves" regarding Plaintiff's concerns, and instructing faculty not to speak with Plaintiff, deny Plaintiff the right to free speech under the first amendment to the Constitution of the United States as applied to the State of Ohio by the fourteenth amendment to the Constitution of the United States. In addition, Defendants' actions and policies undertaken pursuant to the laws, customs, usages, and practices of the state of Ohio are, therefore, unconstitutional and unlawful pursuant to 42 U.S.C. § 1983.

## COUNT FOUR

57. Plaintiff repeats and realleges the allegations of paragraphs 1 through 55, as set forth herein in their entirety and makes the same a part hereof by reference thereto.

58. Defendants' actions, including, but not limited to, inquiring into Plaintiff's animal rights beliefs, instructing Plaintiff not to "make waves" regarding Plaintiff's concerns, and instructing faculty not to speak with Plaintiff, deny Plaintiff the right to free speech under Article I, section 11 of the Constitution of the State of Ohio.

## COUNT FIVE

59. Plaintiff repeats each and every allegation contained in paragraphs 1 through 57, as set forth herein in their entirety and makes the same a part hereof by reference thereto.

60. Defendants' actions, including, but not limited to, inquiring into Plaintiff's animal rights beliefs, instructing Plaintiff not to "make waves" regarding Plaintiff's concerns, and instructing faculty not to speak with Plaintiff, deny Plaintiff the right to free association under the first amendment to the Constitution of the United States as applied to the State of Ohio by the fourteenth amendment to the Constitution of the United States. In addition, Defendants' actions and policies undertaken pursuant to the laws, customs, usages, and practices of the state

of Ohio are, therefore, unconstitutional and unlawful pursuant to 42 U.S.C. § 1983.

## COUNT SIX

61. Plaintiff repeats and realleges the allegations of paragraphs 1 through 59, as set forth herein in their entirety and makes the same a part hereof by reference thereto.

62. Defendants' actions, including, but not limited to, inquiring into Plaintiff's animal rights beliefs, instructing Plaintiff not to "make waves" regarding Plaintiff's concerns, and instructing faculty not to speak with Plaintiff, deny Plaintiff the right to free association under Article I, section 3 of the Constitution of the State of Ohio.

## COUNT SEVEN

63. Plaintiff repeats each and every allegation contained in paragraphs 1 through 61, as set forth herein in their entirety and makes the same a part hereof by reference thereto.

64. Defendants' denial to Plaintiff of an educational alternative to the surgery course 620/21 requirements despite her religious and moral beliefs, and Defendants' consequent violation of Plaintiff's fundamental rights, violate the due process clause of the fourteenth amendment to the United States Constitution. In addition, Defendants' actions and policies undertaken pursuant to the laws, customs, usages, and practices of the state of Ohio are, therefore, unconstitutional and unlawful pursuant to 42 U.S.C. § 1983.

## COUNT EIGHT

65. Plaintiff repeats each and every allegation contained in paragraphs 1 through 63, as set forth herein in their entirety and makes the same a part hereof by reference thereto.

66. The actions of the Defendants, individually and collectively, violate the fourteenth amendment to the United States Constitution, in that they have deprived, and are continuing to deprive, Plaintiff of her property interest in her education, of

her liberty interests in her reputation, standing, and future educational and career opportunities, all without procedural due process. Defendants' refusal to accommodate Plaintiff's religious and moral beliefs, and refusal to undertake reasonable alternative studies and actions penalizing her were based on unlawful, irrelevant, unfounded and arbitrary and capricious criteria.

67. This deprivation of Plaintiff's property and liberty interests occurred as a result of Defendants' failure to consider the religious and moral nature of Plaintiff's beliefs and objections to vivisection and the possibility and value of alternative assignments. In addition, Defendants' actions and policies undertaken pursuant to the laws, customs, usages, and practices of the State of Ohio are, therefore, unconstitutional and unlawful pursuant to 42 U.S.C. § 1983.

### COUNT NINE

68. Plaintiff repeats each and every allegation contained in paragraphs 1 through 65, as set forth herein in their entirety and makes the same a part hereof by reference thereto.

69. Defendants' refusal to provide Plaintiff an alternative, despite her religious and moral beliefs, and discriminatory actions towards Plaintiff based on her religious and moral beliefs, and in light of Defendants' differential treatment of other students constitutes an impermissible burden on her first amendment rights, and as such, creates a state classification of discrimination against students with her religious and moral beliefs. Such classification violates Plaintiff's equal protection rights under the fourteenth amendment of the Constitution of the United States.

Defendants' actions and policies undertaken pursuant to the laws, customs, usages, and practices of the State of Ohio are, therefore, unconstitutional and unlawful pursuant to 42 U.S.C. § 1983.

### COUNT TEN

70. Plaintiff repeats each and every allegation contained in paragraphs 1 through 68, as set forth herein in their entirety

118

and makes the same a part hereof by reference thereto.

71. Defendants' refusal to provide Plaintiff an alternative, despite her religious and moral beliefs, and Defendants' discriminatory actions towards Plaintiff based on her religious and moral beliefs, constitutes an impermissible burden on her first amendment rights, and as such, creates a state classification of discrimination against students with her religious and moral beliefs. Such classification violates Plaintiff's equal protection rights under Article II, Section 26 of the Ohio Constitution.

## COUNT ELEVEN

72. Plaintiff repeats each and every allegation contained in paragraphs 1 through 70, as set forth herein in their entirety and makes the same a part hereof by reference thereto.

73. Defendants' denial to Plaintiff of an educational alternative to the course 620/21 curriculum because of her religious and moral beliefs, violates the contract between Plaintiff and Defendants, in which Plaintiff has paid money in exchange for an education that is nondiscriminatory and respectful of a student's religious and moral principles. By making decisions about Plaintiff's education that were not based on Plaintiff's best interest or any legitimate interests that Defendants may have, and by instead making decisions based on animus against Plaintiff because of her sincerely held religious and moral beliefs, Defendants have violated their contract with Plaintiff.

## COUNT TWELVE

74. Plaintiff repeats each and every allegation contained in paragraphs 1 through 73, as set forth herein in their entirety and makes the same a part hereof by reference thereto.

75. Defendants' assurances in the early summer that an alternative would be made available within a reasonable period of time and would likely be in place before the end of Plaintiff's third year, reasonably induced Plaintiff to rely on those promises to her detriment, thus making Defendants liable to Plaintiff under a promissory estoppel theory.

## COUNT THIRTEEN

76. Plaintiff repeats each and every allegation contained in paragraphs 1 through 74, as set forth herein in their entirety and makes the same a part hereof by reference thereto.

77. Defendant Wyman's blatant failure to fulfill his designated responsibility to act as a student advocate on behalf of Plaintiff, and his failure to ensure that productive and meaningful lines of communication are maintained between students, faculty and administration, and that students' problems are addressed in a meaningful manner, constitutes a violation of Defendant's contractual obligations to Plaintiff.

## COUNT FOURTEEN

78. Plaintiff repeats each and every allegation contained in paragraphs 1 through 76, as set forth herein in their entirety and makes the same a part hereof by reference hereto.

79. Defendant Wyman's conduct, including, but not limited to, his harassment of Plaintiff, through public ridicule of her deeply held religious and moral beliefs, and his disclosure to other students of information about Plaintiff made confidential under federal law, has been motivated by an intent to retaliate against Plaintiff for the free expression of her deeply held religious and moral beliefs, by an animus toward Plaintiff's religious and moral beliefs, and for the purpose of chilling her expression of such beliefs, and has caused, and continues to cause, Plaintiff emotional harm, embarrassment, and ridicule.

## COUNT FIFTEEN

80. Plaintiff repeats each and every allegation contained in paragraphs 1 through 78, as set forth herein in their entirety and makes the same a part hereof by reference hereto.

81. Defendant Wyman's conduct, including, but not limited to, his disclosure of information about Plaintiff's educational status without express permission from Plaintiff violates 20 U.S.C. § 1232g, and is actionable under 42 U.S.C. § 1983.

120

**WHEREFORE,** Plaintiff requests this Court to:

(1)   declare that the actions of the Defendants denied Plaintiff the right to free exercise of religion under the first amendment of the United States Constitution and Article I, section 11 of the Ohio Constitution, and are, therefore, unconstitutional and void;

(2)   declare that the actions of the Defendants denied Plaintiff the right to free speech under the first amendment of the Constitution of the United States, and Article I, Section 11 of the Ohio State Constitution;

(3)   declare that the actions of the Defendants denied Plaintiff the right to free association under the first amendment of the Constitution of the United States, and Article I, Section 3 of the Ohio State Constitution;

(4)   declare that the actions of the Defendants denied Plaintiff the right to due process under the fourteenth amendment of the Constitution of the United States;

(5)   declare that the actions of Defendants denied Plaintiff the right to equal protection under the fourteenth amendment of the Constitution of the United States and Article 2, Section 26 of the Ohio State Constitution;

(6)   declare that the Defendants violated their contractual relationship with Plaintiff to provide a nondiscriminatory education which is respectful of her religious and moral principles, and breached their promise to provide Plaintiff with an alternative within a reasonable period of time, knowing Plaintiff would rely upon this promise, and which promise Plaintiff did reasonably rely upon to her detriment;

(7)   declare that Defendant Wyman's actions have caused, and are continuing to cause, Plaintiff emotional harm, embarrassment, and ridicule;

(8)   direct Defendants to provide Plaintiff an alternative to using, harming, and killing healthy animals and to provide full credit to Plaintiff for the course 620/21 curriculum upon her completion of that alternative;

(9) enjoin temporarily and permanently, the Defendants from failing Plaintiff as a result of her refusal to complete course 620/21 or to participate in the actions to which Plaintiff objects on sincerely held religious and moral grounds;

(10) enjoin temporarily and permanently, the Defendants from imposing on Plaintiff any penalty of any kind as a result of her refusal to complete course 620/21 or to participate in the actions to which Plaintiff objects on sincerely held religious and moral grounds;

(11) direct Defendants to rectify and remove, or other-wise refrain from including, penalties or comments from Plaintiff's academic record resulting from her religious and moral objection to the current 620/21 surgery lab requirements;

(12) award Plaintiff compensatory and punitive damages;

(13) award Plaintiff attorneys fees and costs; and

(14) direct other relief as this Court deems just and equitable.

Respectfully submitted,

_____

Kathaleen B. Schulte (0031448)
SPATER, GITTES, SCHULTE & KOLMAN
723 Oak Street
Columbus, Ohio  43205
(614) 221-1160

Trial Attorney for Plaintiff

**Of Counsel:**

Gary L. Francione
Professor of Law
Rutgers Law School
15 Washington Street
Newark, New Jersey 07102
(201) 648-5989

## JURY DEMAND

Pursuant to Federal Rules of Civil Procedure 38(b) and 39, Plaintiff hereby demands a trial by jury as to all issues triable by jury.

_____

Kathaleen B. Schulte

# Appendix III

## American Bar Association
## Young Lawyers Division (YLD)
## Committee on Animal Protection Law

### RECOMMENDATION

BE IT RESOLVED, That the American Bar Association urges that elementary and secondary schools, colleges and universities, and professional schools not require as a condition of graduation or as a condition of receiving full credit for a required course that a student engage in vivisection of an animal when such action would violate the student's sincerely held religious or moral beliefs, and further urges that these educational institutions strive to provide such a student with a morally acceptable alternative.

### REPORT

I. *Background*

In the past decade, social concern for animal welfare has increased dramatically. This concern has become clear in a number of areas, including the use of animals in teaching. Some educational institutions require that students engage in vivisection of animals as a condition of receiving a degree, or as a condition of receiving full credit in a required course. Such requirements have unfortunately led to conflict between educators and students whose religious and moral views about animals preclude their killing a healthy animal, or their causing unnecessary pain to an animal.

For example, in 1986, two students at the University of Pennsylvania School of Veterinary Medicine were given grades of "F" when they refused to engage in a required "dog lab" as part of their introductory surgery course. The lab required that the students perform various surgical exercises on live, healthy dogs, allow the dogs to recover from anesthesia and remain conscious for several days, and then subject the animals to other surgical procedures that would result in the death of the animal. These two students, both of whom had excellent undergraduate and graduate school records, refused to engage in "dog lab" because of their religious and moral beliefs concerning animal welfare. Although a special faculty committee recommended that the students be given a morally acceptable alternative, a larger faculty group refused to approve an alternative and stated that the students would fail the required surgery course if they refused to participate.

After the students were given grades of "F" for failing to participate, the students brought suit in federal court, alleging a violation of their rights under the federal and state constitutions, as well as under various state doctrines involving tort and contract. The School eventually settled and provided an alternative completely acceptable to the students.

Such situations are occurring with considerable frequency all over the United States. Although many of these situations are resolved through the good will of the relevant faculty acting with the student, some lawsuits have occurred, and in some cases, students have been dismissed from educational institutions after refusing to do the required vivisection or dissection.

## II. *Constitutional Status of Such Requirements*

The Supreme Court has long interpreted the free exercise clause of the first amendment to prohibit the state from requiring that an individual engage in conduct that violates the individual's religious or moral beliefs as a condition of receiving a state benefit. *See e.g., Sherbert v. Verner,* 374 U.S. 398 (1963). Where the educational institution is a state school, or a private school that can, for various reasons, be treated as a state actor, the institution arguably cannot require that a student with sincerely held moral or religious views engage in vivisection or dissection as a condition of receiving a degree or full credit for a required course unless the state could show: (1) a compelling state interest; and (2) the requirement favored by the state was the least restrictive alternative. Many states with state constitutional provisions similar to the first amendment have been similarly interpreted by state courts.

In cases of vivisection and dissection in educational contexts, the refutation of the necessity of the activity is clear from the fact that other nations, most notably Britain, have outlawed the use of live animals in teaching (even in medical and veterinary schools) for over one hundred years and no one would say that the training of British scientists, medical doctors, and veterinarians is inferior to the training provided in the United States. Indeed, many prominent faculty members of American medical and veterinary schools were trained in Britain. Moreover, numerous alternatives exist for the relatively small number of students who will request such an option. Finally, it is difficult, if not impossible, even to imagine the necessity for such activity at the elementary, high school, or undergraduate level.

Requiring students to engage in overt acts, such as killing a healthy animal, is clearly different from requiring them to listen to a lecture that contains material that might offend them. In the latter instance, the only harm suffered is that the student is required to think about an issue that the student finds problematic in some sense; in the former, the student is forced to commit an overt act that may violate deeply held religious or moral beliefs.

## III. *General Desirability of Alternatives*

Beyond any legal argument against such requirements is the more general concern for students to pursue their educational careers without being forced to undertake actions that violate sincerely held religious and ethical beliefs, or being required to institute lawsuits to vindicate their legal rights. Concerns for animal welfare are increasing in our society, although some educational institutions are hostile to these concerns.

For example, students have contacted groups like the YLD Animal Protection Committee and the Animal Legal Defense Fund and have reported instances where professors ridicule students in class and accuse them of being "not fit to be scientists" because they will not engage in vivisection in a course context. Universities and professional schools are often reluctant to provide alternatives because of a concern not to promote animal welfare as a political idea. For example, in the lawsuit involving the University of Pennsylvania referred to above, testimony was given to the court by a Vet School professor that although alternatives existed, the school was reluctant to provide them because it wanted to "hold firm" against "animal rights" people.

It is, of course, understandable that those in the scientific community (as well as in the community at large) object to unlawful activities undertaken by a very small portion of those involved in the animal rights movement. But those illegal activities should not lead to a general hysteria about legitimate animal welfare concerns, especially when those concerns are linked so inextricably with concerns for individual human rights.

## IV. *Summary*

This is a modest proposal dealing with the individual rights of students. It does *not* address the separate and different issue concerning the use of animals in biomedical research. It does *not in any way* purport to affect any academic freedom of the instructor to design course requirements. If the instructor wants to impose a course requirement for the vast majority of students who will not object on moral grounds, and that proposal is approved by the faculty, then this proposal would not directly or indirectly suggest the impropriety of such a requirement. This proposal is *not* intended to signify the ABA or the YLD taking a stand on the vivisection questions per se. This proposal would not protect any right of students to object to a course instructor teaching about vivisection, dissection, or any other material that the student found objectionable even on religious or moral grounds. The proposal affects only the right of students not to be forced to engage in *overt actions* that are inimical to their religious and moral beliefs, and where alternatives clearly exist.

Gary L. Francione

# Appendix IV

*California Code, Education Code §§ 32255.1, 3, 4, 5, 6, provide:*

## § 32255. Pupil with moral objection to dissection or otherwise harming or destroying animals; notice; alternative education project

(a) Except as otherwise provided in Section 32255.6, any pupil with a moral objection to dissecting or otherwise harming or destroying animals, or any parts thereof, shall notify his or her teacher regarding this objection, upon notification by the school of his or her rights pursuant to Section 32255.4.

(b) If the pupil chooses to refrain from participation in an education project involving the harmful or destructive use of animals, and if the teacher believes that an adequate alternative education project is possible, then the teacher may work with the pupil to develop and agree upon an alternate education project for the purpose of providing the pupil an alternate avenue for obtaining the knowledge, information, or experience required by the course of study in question.

(c) The alternative education project shall require a comparable time and effort investment by the pupil. It shall not, as a means of penalizing the pupil be more arduous than the original education project.

(d) The pupil shall not be discriminated against based upon his or her decision to exercise his or her rights pursuant to this chapter.

(e) Pupils choosing an alternative educational project shall pass all examinations of the respective course of study in order to receive credit for that course of study. However, if tests require the harmful or destructive use of animals, a pupil may, similarly, seek alternative tests pursuant to this chapter.

(f) A pupil's objection to participating in an educational project pursuant to this section shall be substantiated by a note from his or her parent or guardian.

(Added by Stats.1988, c. 65, § 2.)

### § 32255.3 Decision of teacher on alternative educational project not arbitrary or capricious

(a) A teacher's decision in determining if a pupil may pursue an alternative educational project or be excused from the project shall not be arbitrary or capricious.

(b) Nothing in this chapter shall prevent any pupil from pursuing the grievance procedures in existing law.

(Added by Stats.1988, c. 65, § 2.)

### § 32255.4 Teacher utilizing live or dead animals or parts in course; duty to inform pupils of rights

Each teacher teaching a course that utilizes live or dead animals or animal parts shall also inform the pupils of their rights pursuant to this chapter.

(Added by Stats.1988, c. 65, § 2.)

### § 32255.5 Application of chapter from kindergarten through grades 1 to 12

Notwithstanding any provision of law to the contrary, this chapter applies to all levels of instruction in all public schools operating programs from kindergarten through grades 1 to 12, inclusive.

(Added by Stats.1988, c. 65 § 2.)

### § 32255.6 Exemption of certain classes and activities from chapter

Classes and activities, conducted as part of a program in agricultural education that provide instruction on the care, management, and evaluation of domestic animals are exempt from the provisions of this chapter.

(Added by Stats.1988, c. 65, § 2.)

*Florida Statutes, Education, § 233.0674 provides:*

## 233.0674. Biological experiments on living subjects

**(1) Legislative intent.—**

(a) The Legislature finds that:

1. Biological experimentation is essential for an understanding of the complexity and diversity of life processes;
2. Such studies should lead to a broader awareness of living systems;
3. Capable students anxious to pursue careers in biological sciences should receive appropriate encouragement and guidance; and
4. Biological experimentation should be within the comprehension and capabilities of the student undertaking the study.

(b) The Legislature recognizes that the use of live animals in some kinds of experiments by students in grades K through 12 may be distasteful or traumatizing to immature students.

**(2) State policy.—**It is therefore the intent of the Legislature with respect to biological experiments involving living subjects by students in grades K through 12 that:

(a) No surgery or dissection shall be performed on any living mammalian vertebrate or bird. Dissection may be performed on nonliving mammals or birds secured from a recognized source of such specimens and under supervision of qualified instructors.

Students may be excused upon written request of a parent or guardian.

(b) Lower orders of life and invertebrates may be used in such experiments.

(c) Nonmammalian vertebrates, excluding birds, may be used in biological experiments, provided that physiological harm does not result from such experiments. Anatomical studies shall only be conducted on models which are anatomically correct for the animal being studied or on nonliving nonmammalian vertebrates secured from a recognized source of such specimens and under the supervision of qualified instructors. Students may be excused from such experiments upon written request of the parent of guardian.

(d) Observational studies of animals in the wild or in zoological parks, gardens, or aquaria, or of pets, fish, domestic animals, or livestock may be conducted.

(e) Studies of vertebrate animal cells, such as red blood cells or other tissue cells, plasma or serum, or anatomical specimens, such as organs, tissues, or skeletons, purchased or acquired from biological supply houses or research facilities or from wholesale or retail establishments which supply carcasses or parts of food animals may be conducted.

(f) Normal physiological and behavioral studies of the human animal may be conducted, provided that such projects are carefully selected so that neither physiological or psychological harm to the subject can result from such studies.

(g) All experiments shall be carried out under the supervision of a competent science teacher who shall be responsible for ensuring that the student has the necessary comprehension for the study to be undertaken. Whenever feasible, specifically qualified experts in the field should be consulted.

(h) Live animals on the premises of public and nonpublic elementary and secondary schools shall be housed and cared for in a humane and safe manner. Animals shall not remain on the premises of any school during periods when such school is not in session, unless adequate care is provided for such animals.

**(3) Exemptions.**—The provisions of this section shall not be construed to prohibit or constrain conventional instruction in the normal practices of animal husbandry or exhibition of any livestock in connection with any agricultural program or instruction of advanced students participating in advanced research, scientific studies, or projects.

# About the Authors

Gary L. Francione is Professor of Law at Rutgers—The State University of New Jersey, School of Law, in Newark, New Jersey. He is also Director of the Rutgers Animal Rights Law Clinic, the first of its kind at any law school in the country.

Professor Francione took his B.A. in philosophy from the University of Rochester in 1976, and his M.A. in philosophy from the University of Virginia in 1981. He also received his J.D. degree from the University of Virginia School of Law in 1981, where he was Articles Editor of the *Virginia Law Review.* Professor Francione is a member of both Phi Beta Kappa and Order of the Coif.

Following graduation, Professor Francione served as law clerk to Judge Albert Tate, United States Court of Appeals for the Fifth Circuit, and then to Justice Sandra Day O'Connor of the United States Supreme Court. He practiced law at Cravath, Swaine & Moore in New York City, and then joined the faculty of the University of Pennsylvania Law School in 1984. In July 1989, he was appointed Professor of Law at Rutgers, where he teaches courses in criminal law, torts, administrative law, and animal rights.

Professor Francione has long been active in litigating animal rights cases, and has advised activists and organizations around the country. He was active in the efforts to close the head injury laboratory at the University of Pennsylvania, represented the American Society for the Prevention of Cruelty to Animals in a lawsuit brought against it by members of the Santeria religion that used animals in religious sacrifices, served as General Counsel to People for the Ethical Treatment of Animals, and has represented numerous students who oppose vivisection or dissection in the classroom. He has successfully sued universities in an effort to get access to the meetings and documents of animal care committees.

134

Anna E. Charlton is Associate Director of the Rutgers Animal Rights Law Clinic. Ms. Charlton took her B.A. from the University of Virginia in 1981, and her J.D. degree from the University of Pennsylvania Law School in 1989. She served as Executive Editor of the *University of Pennsylvania Law Review.*

After graduation, she was associated with the law firm of Simpson, Thacher & Bartlett in New York City. She became Associate Director of the Clinic in Spring 1991. She returned to the Clinic in 1992 after taking a one-year leave of absence to serve as law clerk to Judge Leonard Garth, United States Court of Appeals for the Third Circuit.

Ms. Charlton is Vice-Chair of the Animal Protection Committee of the American Bar Association, and Editor of the *Animal Law Reporter.*

For additional information and inquiries, or to support the campaign for student rights in the classroom, or to purchase additional·copies of this book, contact:

The Rutgers Animal Rights Law Clinic
Rutgers University School of Law
15 Washington Street
Newark, New Jersey 07102-3192
(201) 648-5989

The American Anti-Vivisection Society
801 Old York Road, #204
Jenkintown, PA 19046-1685
(215) 887-0816

136